# Mamas Ignited

## Stop Ironing Start Living

Extinguish the pain of fear, trauma and adversity to Ignite your Spark and Surf the Fire.

Written by
**Louisa Herridge**

Disclaimer

I have tried to recreate events, locales and conversations from my memories of them. In order to maintain their anonymity in some instances I have changed the names of individuals and places, I may have changed some identifying characteristics and details such as physical properties, occupations and places of residence.

Copyright © 2022 by Louisa Herridge

ISBN13: 9798403742160

All rights reserved.

No part of this book may be reproduced in any form or by any electronic or mechanical means, including information storage and retrieval systems, without written permission from the author, except for the use of brief quotations in a book review.

# Contents

Foreword   7
About the Author   11

Prologue   13

**Part One**
**Ignite Your Spark**
1. Self   37
2. Positivity   53
3. Affirmations   79
4. Receive   90
5. Kindness   106

**Part Two**
**Surf The Fire**
6. Fear   127
7. Ignite   136
8. Rise   148
9. Empower   161

Epilogue   170
Acknowledgments   176
Useful Links   181

Work With Louisa   182

# Dedication

**This book is dedicated to
Emilie**

*My Baba. My everything.*

*Promise me you will never go to sleep without saying,*

*"Night-night, sweet dreams, I love you, you're the best in the world."*

*Dream big darling. Mama will always be here to chase your dreams with you.*

*You can be anything you want to be.*

# Foreword
## by Jo Swann

I bloody love women on a mission. I'm drawn to them, and them me (it's like fatal attraction except without the death and sex!) but there is that sense of inevitability about it - if you're a passion and purpose fuelled female entrepreneur - it's likely we'll end up in each other's worlds.

Empowering women to share their stories to create a ripple effect of further empowerment often feels like sharing fairy-tales - the 'happy ever after' that follows the 'deep dark times'... and in every fairy-tale there is a heroine.

What I love about Louisa and what she's created with this book is, whilst she is very much the heroine of her own story (something she'll blush at, shrink away from, shrug off) she's also enabling you to be your heroine- in fact that's exactly what she wants!

When we first started working with Louisa her brand didn't exist and I remember so clearly her excitedly telling me she had this spark of an idea, an idea about how she could bring it to life and how she believed it would ignite excitement in those who needed her. I did a *By Jove you've got it* dance in my office as she shared with me her concept and we chatted ironing boards, surfboards and 1950s retro styling... this was a woman who was inspired, this was a woman fired up, this was a woman on a bloody mission. I loved everything about her and it's a huge honour to be introducing her to you today.

So, what else can I tell you about Louisa and what you can expect from this book?

Well - she hates injustice. She has a huge heart. She has a determination like nothing else. She is fabulously loyal and she's a cheerleader for so many other incredible women she supports.

This book has come to life because it was literally burning a hole in her! (Ok well maybe not literally but you get the point) She HAD to write it, she's had it in her for years, but only recently has she allowed herself to take the role of leader to enable her to share all the power in here.

You see, she, as I'm sure she will tell you, has lived a lot of life in her 42 years, but she has at times been on the floor with her confidence, thanks to it being stolen from her. Even last year she was still questioning her place in the world - whether she could really take up the space she wanted to, whether she was credible to spread her message, whether she was worthy...

Well... let me tell you she is MORE than worthy, she is MORE than credible and she is a force to be reckoned with. With Louisa behind you, you can achieve anything.

I am so happy you are reading this book because this could be the beginning for you - whether it's a new venture, whether it's a new start, or whether it's a totally new life you're looking for, with Louisa in your pocket you WILL make changes, you WILL move forward, you WILL stop ironing, start living.

How exciting!

**Jo Swann**

**Chocolate PR**

# About the Author

*"An ironing board is a surfboard that gave up on its dreams and got a boring job."*

Louisa is a Positive Psychology, mindset and empowerment coach. Like the glorious phoenix, she has risen from the ashes of abuse and trauma; reborn in flames as the blazing leader of the *Mamas Ignited* movement, showing all mums that there can be more than the 2.4 and dreams are there for the taking.

Louisa, 42 from Warrington, is an entrepreneurial solo mum who has overcome domestic violence and debt and lived with chronic pain which led to depression and major back surgery. In the last two years, due to a violent assault at the hands of her ex-partner, she is healing from complex trauma and experienced emotional and psychological burnout, before finding and creating a new path in life whilst healing herself and young daughter too.

Following 20 years in leadership, coaching and teaching, Louisa is now on a mission to encourage all women to believe in themselves, to ignite their spark to BE more, DO more and HAVE more. Louisa uses Positive Psychology tools and interventions supporting mindset and mindfulness to motivate and inspire women to create and build their own dream lives whether that be through building personal confidence or creating impact in business.

Louisa, already a Number One best-selling co-author in the collaboration *'Pride - Motivation and Inspiration for women juggling motherhood and business.'* and made waves with her debut *'Time to Ignite - the five-step mindfulness system'* in 2021.

She leads a range of workshops, courses and collaborative projects alongside her one-to-one coaching packages. She works with women wanting to ignite their spark and entrepreneurs to ignite their impact in business.

Louisa is a freelance writer with Chocolate PR and proof-reader with Authors & Co and in May 2022 will launch *From the Ashes; She is Ignited* – A powerful collaborative book that she has co-ordinated.

Louisa is well known for her fun-loving personality and lives out her mission statement... *An Ironing board is a surfboard that gave up on its dreams and got a boring job... don't be an ironing board!*

www.mamasignited.co.uk

# Prologue

*"If you can dream it, you can do it."*

*"All our dreams can come true if we have the courage to pursue them."*

— Walt Disney

Who has time to iron? Definitely not me! There are two camps here... those like me who haven't ironed in years and those who have no clue how us non-ironers get through life. Which camp are you in? I was never destined to be a 1950s housewife type and this stereotype, and the patriarchy, has a whole lot to answer for. But for a long time, I was in search of the 2.4 family. The *Happy Ever After* and my dreams got lost along the way. *Mamas Ignited - Stop Ironing, Start Living* is my story, your story, our story, because we have all at times wanted more... and that NEVER involves more ironing.

Regardless of where you are now in life - employed, self-employed, new in business, side hustle or still dreaming, I know that if you are reading this book that, like me, you want more, and I want you to know that it is there for the taking. We have all played small at times, allowed limiting beliefs to control us or lived to please others.

It stops now.

Over the last eighteen months I have built a business from scratch after pulling myself out of the depths of despair and a vortex of doom. I have reinvented my life to follow this mission and I am proud to be living out my mantra by ditching my ironing board; leaving a teaching career to lead the *Mamas Ignited Movement* - riding my surfboard and fulfilling my soul's purpose to write, speak, coach and empower.

Your ironing board and everything it represents – fear, limiting beliefs, trauma and adversity - will no longer keep you trapped. We are *Mamas Ignited* and together we have the choice to stop ironing and give that board its true destiny... to be a surfboard and surf the fire of life with passion and purpose.

This book is for:

- The woman that is ready to change her *mindset*.
- The woman who has been *hiding* for way too long and is ready to *ignite her spark*.
- The woman who wants to add more *fire* to her life and business.
- The woman that wants to stop seeking love and validation and the need to please.
- The woman who has lost her desire to *surf* but wants so much more from life.

Grab your board, stop ironing, start living and let's hit the waves of success together!

## The Climb

At age twenty-five, I was on the top of the world. At least it felt like it. I was at the top of the Sydney Harbour Bridge – a climb that everything inside me told me I couldn't do. Twenty-five years of limiting beliefs told me that I couldn't do it; that it was too dangerous. In that moment, as I stood at the very top with my arms stretched wide, I knew that I could achieve anything in life. I'd been held back for far too long.

Australia was pivotal. Age twenty-five was pivotal. I had finally flown the nest, cut the apron strings, and done something for ME. I had travelled to the opposite side of the world, something that I had wanted to do after university, but as I'd been discouraged so much from going backpacking, I didn't have the confidence to just go for it.

Up until the age of twenty-four, I did what I was *supposed* to do. I did well at school, I worked hard, I went to university, got a degree, I had a boyfriend, I got engaged, I bought a house. I did what was expected of me – expected by who? Society? My parents? I'm not sure. I was a people-pleaser and instead of following my wanderlust and my authentic truth, I played safe. I had stayed local for university and had felt obliged to come home every week, for my boyfriend, for my family – so, I only half-left home and never felt that I was fully self-sufficient.

My university hangover hit me hard. I missed the Louisa that I was when away from home, I missed the learning, the freedom, and the endless possibilities. When I came to the end of my degree, I hadn't a clue what happened next, so I applied for a Masters. As a natural academic, I felt at home at university. The course, TV & Radio Scriptwriting, was only offered part-time so I needed to get a job. The two-year MA fulfilled the creative yearn that I'd had my whole life and, for the first time, I was free to write, to create, to imagine... and I loved it. One day a week, I was alive and my authentic self, the rest I was being the good girl, the conformist.

For two years, I lived in a limbo life. Age twenty-two, I was ready to step into the world of media. I had the talent, ambition and desire to go for it. Scripts were being sent off to BBC and ITV, I was winning writing competitions, I was working in London as a runner for several TV companies and I even applied for presenting jobs getting down to the last fifteen for a spot hosting a segment with Princess productions. I was alive.

That's when *Sliding Doors* came into play (remember the film with Gwyneth Paltrow?) These unwritten rules and expectations of life were hanging over me - I should be getting engaged, buying a house, getting married and having a baby. That's what everyone around me was doing - school friends, university friends and I was the odd one out. At this point, the 2.4 was far from my mind but I had a boyfriend and we had moved in together, I had a good job as a Team Leader in a call centre, but I was so much happier when I was writing or working on TV projects – the truth was, I wanted *more* and I knew that I was capable of so *much more*.

It wasn't Bridgerton. I wasn't living for marriage, yet there was something unwritten that made me feel like I had to aspire to marriage. He was offering me the prescribed life; he was my gentleman caller, and he was offering me a very fair proposal and one that I'd be a fool to refuse. So, I accepted.

I always felt that he didn't like me working away, having ambition and the truth is, we were growing apart long before we finally broke up. He didn't make me choose between my career and him. But I was made to choose. Who made me choose? I'm not sure, but I can remember the Louisa who sat at her PC writing, who imagined a world of media, TV, writing and presenting. The young woman of twenty-two who still had the same ambitions as her fourteen-year-old self who knew that she didn't want to settle down. I can still picture these *sliding doors* worlds vividly. The happily married 2.4 life or the excitement and adventure of career and travel? I know which one that I truly wanted. I also know which one I chose.

At the same time, the universe threw me a curve ball and I injured my back. My bad back ensured that my dreams of moving to London, at that point, were quashed and for a while, I lived the 2.4 life - buying a flat, getting engaged whilst recovering from the back injury.

Less than a year later, at the age of twenty-four, after the break-up of my parents, I left the relationship that I had been in since I was seventeen and ran. I ran from the pain from my parent's volatile relationship, the trauma of living though this and I ran away from a life where I no longer knew who I was or what I wanted.

Firstly, I ran away for a summer of fun, a summer working in Majorca as a holiday rep. From there, two months travelling Oz. The world was at my feet. For twenty-four years I had tried to please other people, to do the right thing, to follow the rules and to play safe. That year helped me to escape but by running away, all that I did was bury the feelings, the trauma and pain which I am still healing from now, eighteen years later.

As I stood at the top of that bridge, following the skyline across to the infamous Opera house, I was so proud. I thought about the lady who helped me to conquer this fear. Whilst travelling, I'd met a couple at Ayers Rock who had climbed the Sydney Bridge; it was on her bucket list and finally, at the age of eighty, she had ticked it off. There I was, twenty-five and already with such limiting beliefs telling me that I couldn't do it. I didn't have a fear of heights so there was no reason why I couldn't do it, yet I was so determined that I wouldn't do it until I met that lady. As I heard her speak about the joy that this achievement had brought her, I knew not only that I could do it, but I must. I promised her that I would, and I did. When I reached that summit, I smiled through the tears and was so grateful for the lesson that she had taught me.

As I climbed that bridge, the terror gripped me, my inner demons told me I couldn't do it, but I dug deep and knew that it was just my inner voice trying to stop me. Twenty-five years of feeling afraid to stand out, to be brave, to be my authentic self, evaporated. The euphoria of reaching that highest point lives with me now and although, over the years, my inner demon has got the better of me, I have always known deep down that I could achieve anything that I set my mind to.

The fears that were stopping me climbing that bridge were the same limiting beliefs that stopped me following my career dreams and stopped me going for what I wanted in life.

My need to please and to play it safe have often shown up in my relationships since and so, sadly for a long time, I lost the Louisa from the top of the Bridge. I stayed at the bottom of the bridge, safe and protected.

Not anymore.

## Feeling the Fear

Fear is the strongest form of control and one that often limits us, as that control is often self-inflicted.

Imagine you were climbing that bridge - even though you know it's safe, you are harnessed in, and it has been tested, you physically can't push forward to walk across that bridge. But it is not your physical body that is stopping you, it is your emotional fear.

Fear stops you.

Fear can paralyse you, even though deep down, you might be questioning if what you're scared about really warrants such fear.

Usually, fear stops us to keep us safe, but now, in 2022, we are not fighting sabre tooth tigers with our bare hands and fighting to survive. We have to deal with our rational v irrational brain and the fears that often hold us back, to keep us in an assumed safe place.

Fear often comes from our fear of failure. Throughout our lives, the word *fail* fills us with so much fear and can often hold us back from doing things that we want to do. From an early age, we are surrounded with the notion of *pass or fail* at school, college, driving, lessons, job interviews... but do we ever really fail? The answer is no! But the fear that we attach to that notion can be debilitating.

Fear of failure. Fear of judgement, Fear of success, Fear of being a failure!

We label ourselves *'failure'* when we should be much kinder to ourselves. For a long time, I thought of myself as a failure in love and relationships and at times, a failure as a teacher, failure as a mum... and this was when I was living in my negative mindset. Bad luck came in threes... and the rest!

Two years ago, I felt like a failure in every part of my life. The day my car failed its MOT, the final straw landed on my back. I'd shouldered everything with a smile for six months since I was attacked... but in truth, I'd been battling with trauma for over ten years.

Failing the MOT was the final straw and I broke. In front of a class of 31 Year 11 pupils. I reached rock bottom and was emotionally and psychologically burnt out. I was the lowest I could ever imagine being.

That was the best thing that could have happened to me. I didn't break. I didn't break down. I reached the lowest point and finally allowed myself to reach out for help. To stop faking being okay. To stop smiling, keeping calm and carrying on.

The only way was up.

My life is now an ongoing climb of growth and the view at the top is getting brighter, better, and even more euphoric.

I want you to join me on this climb, to start at the bottom, to break through the fears, take a step past your limiting beliefs to reach the summit of your potential both for your 'self' and for your personal life, relationship and business/career.

# Prologue

If you are reading this book, then I'm assuming that, like me, you have felt held back by fear or limiting beliefs, have experienced adversity or are living with trauma. There may be something in your life that you want to change: your job, house, relationship. You may already have your own business or are ready to switch up your side hustle to create a business, a movement, something that inspires and impacts others. Don't let that fear stop you.

You may have been following my journey and have no interest in starting a business (yet), even so, I know that my story will resonate with you. Whatever way, I am so happy that you are here, and I can't wait to be a part of your journey. Maybe you don't know if you want to do more, maybe you haven't even considered it yet. Perhaps you don't know what is holding you back but my using a combination of my story, business knowledge and coaching methods I will give you the tools to be able to extinguish fear and the pain of the past to feel empowered to create an ignited life.

Or, at the other end of the scale, you might be reading this as someone who is already making impact; this is amazing – but there is always room for *more*!

Self-sabotage, limiting beliefs, fear, inner critics, and procrastination are the undercurrents waiting to knock you off your surfboard, but together we will ignite your spark and get you ready to turn your ironing board into a surfboard and surf through the fires that life sends your way.

So now that we have decided that you are ready for more. You want to be more, do more and have more in your life. You want to put your fears to one side and embrace your full purpose and potential. What is stopping you? Are you not getting as visible as you'd like and feel yourself holding back? Are the inner demons stopping you from showing up?

Ask yourself, have you visualised your success and are you truly open to finding true abundance, or is there a money mindset block or an underlying fear of success? Until last year, I didn't realise that I had both, and both have held me back for a long time.

Think about your life as it is now, do you fear rejection or judgement from others? This was massive for me as I felt so judged within my teaching profession. I couldn't even tell my English teacher colleagues that I had written a book for fear of their judgement – how sad is that?

Perhaps you fear being imperfect... were you one of those girls at school that had to have the neat headline and bubble writing and would rip a page out if you made a mistake? Maybe you procrastinate and are still playing small even though, in your heart, you know that you have the passion and knowledge to be right at the top.

Are you not charging your truth worth? Do you still feel uncomfortable when it comes to valuing your time, knowledge and expertise?

I have answered YES to all of these questions in the last twelve months. It has taken a lot of time, work and determination, and it has not been easy, but I knew that I was worthy of more. I still want more, to do more and have more, without apology.

It all starts with a change of mindset.

## Don't be an Ironing Board

I've said it before, and I will say it again - grab your ironing board, get ready to surf the waves as an *ironing board is just a surfboard that gave up on its dreams and got a boring job.*

Have you ever heard the expression before? When I first read that meme, I almost leapt out of my seat. Don't be an Ironing Board – YES. This summed up how I'd felt for a lot of my life for not following my dreams and instead getting a safe job and searching for the non-existent, perfect 2.4 life.

I left university full of passion and drive to be a journalist, researcher, writer and ended up working in a call centre. With a loss in confidence due to severe health restrictions, and no media opportunities landing at my feet, I gave up on the dream, set up my ironing board and became an English teacher! The phrase that has haunted me since then is *Those who can, do; those who can't, teach.* I proved this to be wrong by having a highly successful sixteen-year career in teaching and leadership... but that fire and passion to write was never fully extinguished and lay dormant inside for far too long. Is that fire inside you too?

The universe is a funny old thing. Somehow by surviving a six-year abusive relationship, complex trauma and recovery from emotional burnout, I have finally managed to board my surfboard and I am riding the waves. Dreams of writing and being published, that had been buried many years ago, have been reignited and the passion that is burning inside of me is beyond words. I want you to feel how I feel. Don't be the ironing board. Find your surfboard and come and join me on the waves of life.

## Ride the wave

As a mindset and empowerment coach, I am on a mission to empower women that do not love the life they are living to join me and ride the wave! I work with women to help them to find their spark - whether that be personally or in their businesses - so that they can turn up the dial on living lives they actually love, transforming their ironing boards into surfboards that will ride the waves of their next adventure!

Let's face it... even without a global pandemic, Mum-life is hard! Relationships are hard! Life is hard! Whether you are single or with a partner; with or without help - we are all doing it all and at times, it feels impossible.

After a violent assault and escaping an abusive relationship, my self-care was at an all-time low.

Living with complex trauma, I was trying to be wonder woman, spinning all the plates and putting on the *'I am fine'* act. I wasn't taking care of myself, couldn't ask for help, struggled to tell people how hard it was. My mental health declined, and I hit rock bottom. Speaking out about mental health and asking for help, as an independent woman, was hard. It took for me to breakdown in tears and have a panic attack in front of a class of 30 Year 11 pupils for me to accept that I needed help.

## Ignite your Spark & Surf the Fire

In the last eighteen months, I have completely transformed from depressed, anxious schoolteacher, feeling all the mum-guilt of juggling full-time teaching and being a solo mum, to creating my own thriving coaching business. Meaning that I can work my business around being mum, and my mental health is the best it has been in years! Plus, I am finally living out my dream of writing for a living, both as an author and freelance writer.

I quit teaching in the middle of a pandemic! Sounds crazy, right? But like many people, the pandemic was the final catalyst for change. So, how did I go from high school teacher, with a well-established 'ironing board life', to Number One best-selling author, motivational speaker and a successful mindset and empowerment coach, inspiring women from all stages of life and business in less than a year?

This book will give you the full insight into how I created and ignited my business and how I made impact within six months of launching *Mamas Ignited*.

It all started when I changed my mindset and became purposeful in my thinking and actively made the decision to be positive, to let go of the fear and give myself permission to be more. It was taking a step into the realms of intentional thinking and growth mindset that shifted my world.

In the last few years, I have dug deep, confronted my fears and trusted that I could make a difference; believed that I could inspire other women, other mamas to ignite their lives; taken action to make sure that I created impact and, by following my passion and purpose, I have done just that.

I did this by investing in ME, both financially, emotionally and for the first time, following my instinct and doing what I wanted to do and not taking the safe, good girl approach to life. I took a chance and I backed myself.

I have made strategic business decisions, some by listening to my gut alone. I have invested in me and in doing so, developed my mindfulness practices by working with world class mentors and immersed myself in an online tribe of positivity and calm. I want this for you.

I have surrounded myself with a powerhouse group of coaches and mentors and I have learned how to show up as the real me, without apology. My mission is driven by my story, and I want to help you to tap into your story and be able to speak from the scar, not the wound; to use your story to ignite your business.

I have had my share of adversity and know how hard it can be to stop listening to your inner critic, voice of doom and the tight grip of imposter syndrome and anxiety. I understand your fear of judgement or failure; I had it too.

I want you to know that you can choose to be more, do more and in turn, have more.

You have infinite possibilities.

## Think Yourself Up

A few years ago, I would have had major imposter syndrome about writing this book – who would want to read my story? But as my friends will confirm, I tell a good tale and I have had my fair share of dramas, adversities and compromising situations over the years.

For sixteen years I was a teacher and so often my family and partners would tell me off for treating them like a pupil. I never intend to, but I suppose it comes with the job. I instinctively want to help others, to offer advice, to coach and to be a mentor. I have tutored, aka coached, hundreds of people over the years and, back in my call centre days as a Team Leader, coaching was my main role. Yet, as I started this journey in coaching, I found it hard to say I was a coach or mentor - after all, I didn't have a qualification. That limiting belief was screaming in my ear – *you are not good enough* - when in fact, I have been coaching and mentoring teaching staff, colleagues and pupils for twenty years.

Let's reframe that thinking: how could I not support, coach and mentor other women when I have had so much success and helped so many people to reach their full potential, when I have so much to share, not just in business but through my truth, my story... and that is the key – mentoring people to find their SPARK.

My limiting beliefs still tap me on the shoulders and in a recent 121 with Amie Blayney, I told her this! She laughed at me. *"Erm, how long were you a teacher? Your 'teacherness' brings the best out of people...you are a coach... Louisa you are a fucking Rockstar!"* I've never been called that before... so I am taking it and running!

I have overcome multiple narcissistic relationships and lived with chronic pain for eight years, which led to depression and major back surgery. In the last two years, due to a violent assault at the hands of my ex-partner, I am living with complex trauma and experienced emotional and psychological burnout, which was the catalyst for creating *Mamas Ignited* and this new authentic, purposeful life. I found my way back to that *sliding door* to follow a new path in life, helping others and helping myself and my daughter to heal in the process.

In November 2020, I achieved finally my dream of being a published author, achieving a Number One Amazon best-seller with my debut collaboration in *'Pride - Motivation and Inspiration for women juggling motherhood and business.'* collated by

Jane Louise Pattison. I went on to publish my first book *'Time to Ignite'* - the five-step mindfulness system in April 2021 and alongside this book I am launching a very special book collaboration in May 2022 – *'From the Ashes; She is Ignited'*.

Working with world class public speaking coach Dani Wallace as one of the headline speakers at Bee Inspired, April 2021 gave me my first big platform to create a happening and from there, my speaking credentials have increased, including Keynote speaker with global company TP Women International, Clear Path Conference - alongside Caroline Strawson - supporting survivors of domestic abuse.

My signature *Ignite* courses and one-to-one packages allow me to be able to work with women from all aspects of life and business, from mindfulness and vision boards to mindset and business impact. I run strategy days and have created a network of clients that support each other to ignite their spark. Self-development is key and I continue to expand my learning through courses and masterminds.

One nugget that I'd like to share is one that I found on a masterclass with Awena Naomi Ella - *Think Yourself Up*. If you think small you will stay small; if you visualise yourself at the top of your game and as a worthy contender in your niche, you will find your seat.

Within a few months in business, I was partnering with and working alongside big names, recognised brands, and holding my own. These strategic moves gave me the kudos and respect from fellow entrepreneurs and not only helped to position me, but also to continue to believe in myself and strive for more. These connections were all important to my business and what I chose to do was *Think myself up*. There was no reason why I couldn't sit at the same table as these formidable women and there's no reason why you can't join us!

This book will take you, in part autobiographically, through my life from ironing board to surfboard, through my learnings and challenges, interweaved with my SPARK and FIRE systems. By following my journey and sharing my learnings, you will be able to see the simple but effective steps needed to step into your personal power and to be able to grow and create a purposeful life and business. By the end of the book, you will have more self-awareness and renewed confidence in yourself and your vision. You will be clear and in control, with passion and purpose for your business and life. This could be by igniting your message and mission, becoming more visible, or taking your first step to reinvent your life and business.

## Mamas Ignited

The first time that someone told me that I inspired them was very difficult to believe. When I was at my lowest and during the most difficult times, I found it so hard to reach out for help. In June 2020, I penned my story of survival and starting a business in my first book, as a part of a collaboration. This changed everything. I shared the difficult story of surviving an abusive relationship, having a break down and going through the court process. By the time this book was published in November 2020, I had already begun to speak out, to get visible and I knew that I wanted *more*. Soon after, more women began to reach out to me; I stepped into this power and acknowledged that I had a purpose bigger than me that I had to share.

*Mamas Ignited* was born in December 2020 and since then, I have made it my mission to empower other women. I have worked with women in business who needed to find and set their non-negotiables, I have championed women to grab their surfboards and begin their own inspiring businesses.

As my visibility increased and my message of the surfboard grew, I began to create a movement. People began to recognise not only my *Mamas Ignited* brand, but the primal code branding of the ironing board. As surfing the ironing board became synonymous with *Mamas Ignited* and well-established coaches began to recognise who I was, I knew that I was onto something. Instilling that belief in so many women; showing that you don't have to put up with a life that you don't love has become my soul purpose and as my own adventure has developed, women in business have begun to follow my journey too.

Now just over a year since *Mamas Ignited* was established, I have inspired hundreds of women to allow themselves to want to be more and do more and the next step is to actively show you HOW to BE more, DO more and unapologetically have more. I know that I have not yet reached the summit of my bridge climb, but to the women in business who are only a few steps behind me, I am here to reach out a hand to you and guide you to the top.

Being featured in the media, podcasts and on global platforms, from Stylist and Thrive Global to the India National Herald and Brooklyn Café TV, I have made impact at every step of my journey. My clients and followers are loyal and are a part of my *Mamahood*. Seeing women's lives transform, and knowing that I have played a part in that, is both humbling and thrilling in equal measure. If you have only just joined my *Mamahood*, then I want you to know that this is only the beginning. I don't do things by halves.

## Ignite Your Spark and Find your Fire

Self-sabotage, childhood experiences and unhealthy relationships leave us in a state of *Fight, Flight, Freeze and Fawn*, and having lived in a trauma response for most of my life, I know the debilitating impact this can have. January 2020, I was broken, I was living in a vortex of doom until I began to research narcissism. Until that point it was a word that I'd never fully understood, but as I lay on the sofa with greasy hair and pyjamas disguised as clothes from the school run, I began to listen to an audio book on narcissism. Things began to come clear. Until then, I'd only been functioning for my daughter; dead inside, filled with darkness. As I came to understand narcissism, my life started to make sense. The painful experiences, the destructive relationships, the abuse, the guilt, the confusion all started to resonate strongly, but from more than one relationship in my life.

**Part One – IGNITE YOUR SPARK** will take you through this transformation with me. I will share the learning and tools that I have discovered and used to empower myself, and to validate any painful experiences and trauma that you may be carrying, whether that be childhood experiences, negative and abusive relationships, grief, health scares, chronic pain - these can all cause trauma which manifests in your mind and body as pain, depression and anxiety. I will take you on a journey of self-discovery so that you can turn your ironing board into a surfboard with me. *Trigger warning – Support links provided at the end of the book.*

**SELF** – Self-esteem, self-awareness, limiting beliefs and reframes.

**POSITIVITY** – Going beyond your adversity, using positive mindset as the key to your success.

**AFFIRMATION** – Positive self-talk and affirmations for mindset.

**RECEIVE** – The power of the Law of Attraction, vision boards and money mindset.

**KINDNESS** – Burnout, non-negotiables, visualisation, meditation, and journaling.

**Part Two – SURF THE FIRE** will show you how you can be reborn, like the phoenix rising from the ashes to bring your sparks to life and ignite your ideas into flames of glory. Together, we will smash through the blocks that are holding you back so that you are ready to surf the waves of success, to overcome fears and limiting beliefs, to ignite, rise from the ashes and live an empowered life.

**FEAR** – Overcoming and smashing your fears by getting in view.

**IGNITE** – Finding your spark, passion, and purpose to set your message on fire.

**RISE** – Sharing your passion with the right people and using your story to make waves.

**EMPOWER** – Creating the ripple effect through connection.

## Grab your Surfboard

No matter what your fears and adversity, despite struggles with mental health, limiting beliefs or trauma, get ready for personal growth, to feel empowered and ready to smash through those blocks and create a glorious plan for your future.

To conquer fear, we need courage and also to find more knowledge. Ask yourself... is what you are afraid of really that bad? Or has someone or something in your past planted that fear? Is the information correct or is your inner voice telling you something that we need to reprogramme?

You don't have to be brave alone... you don't have to find the courage and knowledge alone, find people who are open to having those conversations with you. Find people who want to ask those questions too.

Feel like it's too late? It's never too late to decide you want more from life. To admit to yourself that you have been stood behind your ironing board for too long or don't want to be controlled by fear any more is tough. It's not easy, but will it be worth it? Yes!

It's time to stop being controlled by the fears being planted in us from childhood, bad relationships, society and the media and to tap into what your purpose is, what makes you tingle with passion and excitement, and to get out there and do it.

Join me as I take you through my journey from ironing board to surfboard and impact that continues to make ripples.

Like mine, your climb may, at times, seem impossible or a step too far, but the feeling when you reach the top is beyond words.

You have already taken the first step, now take my hand as we take the next step together.

Let the adventure begin.

# Part One
# Ignite Your Spark

*"Always be the leading lady of your own life."*

— Audrey Hepburn

How many films have you watched over ten times? I grew up watching musicals - Calamity Jane and the Sound of Music being my favourites. Both strong females leads, with, of course, a Hollywood happy ever after. Calamity was my idol and I would be lost in the music, singing 'whip crack away' with all my might.

She reminded me of my Aunty Shirley, who was my real-life idol as she was a professional dancer and toured the world. I wanted to be just like her. The only problem was, I wasn't that good at dancing... no matter how much my parents spent on dance lessons.

Aunty Shirley had, in my mind, an exciting profession and was living her dream and I know that from a young age, I had a spark in me that I wanted to be more. Perhaps this is where my dreaming of more and wanderlust has come from. Hearing her tales of living in exotic countries and cruising filled me with aspirations of a life filled with the same.

Films were a massive part of my childhood and Disney being the biggest part. With my sister Kelly, I watched them on repeat, and when my brother Adam came along, he really had no choice! All of these films had one thing in common – the happy ever after. The usually passive female being saved by finding true love. Now I am not dissing Disney – I am still the biggest fan, but in my day, we didn't have the feisty Rapunzel or the girl-power of Elsa and Anna, and that dream of finding "the one" was implanted. No matter how much we can look to blame the media, it is human nature to want to find a partner and I have seen this from my own daughter planning her own wedding to a variety of boys from the age of four!

Dreams are good. Dreams can come true. But dreams also require action. A fire cannot light itself and once a tiny spark is created, the fire needs fuel and nurture to reach its full potential.

You are the same. You can dream, you can want, but without action, the spark will not light. Join me as I take you through Part One – SPARK, to explore that if you have lost your spark, suffered adversity, rejection or have simply given up hope – how, by taking control to ignite your own spark, you can become the leading lady of your own life and then, my love – anything really is possible!

# Chapter 1
# Self

*"Do one thing you thought you were too afraid to do. Your reward will be a massive boost in self-worth and the feeling of being proud of yourself."*

Let me guess, you are mum, you have a family, a nice house, a good job... but there is something missing? You may be happy in your life and still yearn for more, especially if you are a dreamer. Maybe motherhood has stopped you in your tracks, the pandemic has made you reassess what you really want in life or something that has happened to you means that your life has taken a different direction or been completely derailed. Wherever you are in life... career or no career, qualifications or no qualifications, there is still time for you to grab that surfboard. But perhaps you have lost your true self along the way, lost sight of who you are and what you want in life. So, let's start with that!

I never planned for a family, but in my late twenties I began to yearn for a child. My maternal clock was ticking so loudly, I couldn't concentrate. I don't know at what point in my life I subconsciously understood that to be success in life I had to achieve the 2.4 family. Ambition, school, university and a career in the media was what drove me in my early twenties. But one day, I woke up as a failure. I had the career, the house, the friends, the social life... but I was single. I was thirty, still single, and an utter failure.

No matter how many friends I had, how many job promotions I achieved, how much I travelled the globe, the lack of a partner and baby felt to me like everyone pitied me and I was losing at life.

I was forever the solo one at wedding and parties. I went to countless baby showers and watched my friends from all walks of life - school, university, work - graduate into wifedom and motherhood and there I was, still on the shelf, hurtling towards Miss Havisham.

I preferred to be Bridget. I was a self-confessed Bridget Jones but I used this passive aggressive joke towards myself as a way to shield my pain and to try and avoid the pitying looks of having no plus one *again* by making a joke of it.

That lack of self-esteem from a young age is something that we all can carry with us for the longest of times. The term *Self* covers many areas, namely - *Self-Love, Self-awareness and Self-esteem.*

Self-esteem and confidence... are they the same? Being told things or made to believe certain things impacts us. The year before I started high school, we moved house. We moved to a beautiful four bed detached house, with a double garage! Wow. We loved that house; I still dream about it now. But at the age of eleven, that house became my vice. As an adult, my dad has said, 'One of the worst things we ever did was move to that house as that's where the bullying began.' He was right. It was the first new 'posh estate' in the area and although the rest of Woolston was far from impoverished, with lovely housing estates and parks, this new estate, to my horror named Edward Gardens, was a bridge too far. I was ridiculed, excluded and made to feel an outsider. I yearned to live in one of the 'normal' houses with only one bathroom! I worried about inviting people round, as even the nice friends would comment on the size of the house. I don't wish to sound ungrateful, but I was, unknowingly of course, as when you are in your teens, all you want to do is fit in.

So many people share stories of being bullied and as a teacher I have seen it first-hand in schools. Where do you draw the line between girls squabbling and falling out with it becoming bullying? Add hormones and boys into the mix and things get even more complicated.

Was I called names? Yes. Was I picked on? Yes. Did I ever dread going to school. Yes. Was I bullied? Yes. But I held my own, so is that bullying? Repeated name calling and actively looking to make someone else upset, uncomfortable or sad in my book is bullying. My parents used to say, 'It's just jealousy.' And yes, perhaps it was, but that was never a good enough answer.

I was told to stick up for myself, to make new friends, but my self-esteem and self-love is what took the battering. Even when I moved past the worst, the limiting beliefs remained.

I don't even know myself from high school. If I was fake, true or just doing what I needed to. I was confident in so many ways but hidden in so many others. My true self didn't appear until I went to university. When I left a town where everyone knew me to a neutral place where I could be *me* without my back story, this was where my self-esteem boomed and I stepped into the Louisa that I'd always had the power to be, but I'd been hiding from.

Self-esteem and self-belief are terms that we often use, but do we fully understand the difference and the power that these two things have on our lives and more importantly, the power that we have over our own self-esteem and self-belief?

In its simplest form, self-esteem is the opinion we have of ourselves. If we have high self-esteem, we think positively about ourselves and on the counter, low self-esteem brings negative and critical thinking towards ourselves.

Self-esteem is the overall opinion of yourself as a person. Self-belief, which is equally as important, is your belief in your ability to complete tasks and achieve goals. In business terms, self-belief is the most crucial, but strong self-belief has to be underpinned by high self-esteem.

Limiting beliefs bring about self-sabotage as subconsciously, your brain tries to keep you safe. It tries to keep you safely behind that ironing board so that you don't risk getting hurt.

Think about how self-sabotage stemming from your limiting beliefs shows up in your life.

Do you struggle with trying to get everything right? Do you set standards so high that you exhaust yourself in trying to meet them? Do you procrastinate because you are scared of not doing something perfectly? Do you feel guilty when you make a mistake - even a small one? Do you have trouble relaxing?

You may also find that you have destructive patterns. Do you self-soothe with drugs, food, or alcohol? Do you get involved with inappropriate (including narcissistic) men or women? Do you have toxic friendships?

## Your Own Limiting Beliefs

Our limiting beliefs are like the trunk of a tree. When a tree is chopped down, you can tell the age of the tree by the number of circles, from the very tiniest in the centre as it was a sapling tree, to the huge out rim of the giant oak. This is how I see limiting beliefs. The small inner circles are the tiny little things that happened when you were much younger – being ignored, trying to please your parents, bullying, struggling with maths and being called stupid... these circles get bigger and bigger the older you get, and like the inner circles of the tree's life, they never disappear.

How do your limiting beliefs present now, as an adult? Do you struggle with trying to get everything right? Are you afraid of failing? Do you feel judged by the people around you? Do you procrastinate because you are scared of not doing something perfectly? Do you have impossibly high standards? Do you feel guilty when you make a mistake - even a small one? Does fear stop you doing the things that you really want to do?

## Things that happen 'For you'

Have you heard the expression, *'Things happened for us not to us?'* Until the last year, I was totally unaware of this thinking. I have lived with lots of negativity and whenever anything bad happened, I always had the view that it had happened to me.

Why would I not? I had never even considered that there was another view.

Look back at your life and identify the significant things that have happened you. At the time, these may have been traumatic, painful, and felt very unfair, but if you are anything like me, I know that they will have made you stronger and looking back with what you know now, you will be able to see how far you have come.

Your inner monologue has been forming since childhood and every negative experience since has had an imprint on that circle in your trunk. Now, as an adult, it can be very difficult to separate your true self from those beliefs and sadly, without Doc Brown and his Dolorium, we can never go back and erase those negative moments.

Back to the Future tells us a lot about how our experiences, good and bad, have shaped us. By going back to the past and changing things it changes the future Marty and he begins to fade from the picture. This is the same for our lives, we can look back and regret things and wish we'd done things differently, thought differently or taken a different path, but all of these things happened for us and have brought us to exactly where we are now. If I changed my choices, entered the other part of the *sliding door* or didn't experience the adversities, I wouldn't have Emilie and I wouldn't be writing this book. Although awful at the time, these things do happen for us.

We can't go back and rewrite the past, but what we can do is stop the tree from being felled. We don't need to see the chopped down tree with forty-two rings of past, we need to see the tree standing tall and thriving. Growing taller and stronger to withhold the storms of the next forty-two years! The inner rings are still there, we don't need to see them. Instead, we can grow and by knowing who we are and what has happened for us, we can turn that pain and adversity into strength and power.

We can't change what has happened and the adversity that we may have suffered, but what we can do is positively reframe our thinking and in turn, retrain our belief systems, as a lot of the fears that we hold onto are due to our inner safety alert systems.

## Fight, Flight, Freeze & Fawn

The limbic system categorises human emotions experienced into pleasant or unpleasant mental states, the parasympathetic nervous system acts as our defence system to keep us safe. The amygdala, also known as the animal part, is our internal alarm system and alerts the sympathetic nervous system to any danger or *'perceived danger'*, to trigger the adrenal glands to produce adrenaline. The trigger of the amygdala floods our system with cortisol and adrenalin. So, in simple terms, if faced with real danger, the flood of hormones gives us the power to fight or run away, thus keeping us safe – namely the fight, flight, freeze or fawn system to keep us safe.

Triggers from the amygdala and when the limbic system is on high alert restrict the use of the pre-frontal cortex, also known as the human/rational part of the brain, and so this is why in moments of fear, anxiety, or hysteria, we can't think straight.

This system works on feelings and instinct to keep us safe from danger and instinctive. Memories held in the hippocampus can also trigger the amygdala, as the hippocampus stores our memories and, importantly, feelings associated with a memory, it therefore remembers negative memories and times of not feeling safe to again remind the amygdala that it needs to keep us safe.

Your inner voice can be debilitating at times. It can send you into freeze or flight. This perceived danger is due to limiting beliefs, triggered by your inner voice, which is triggered by your low self-belief.

This is why we need to focus on our self-esteem and self-belief before we even talk in detail about your inner voice. When we let our inner voice take over, we live within the negative and therefore, our self-belief wanes. We begin to ignore our own strengths and focus instead on the weaknesses. We highlight our mistakes and failings to other people and always expect the worst. Due to this low self-belief, we don't accept challenges and avoid situations where we may be stretched or taken out of our comfort zone. Limiting your own belief will inevitably impact your mental state and happiness.

Self-esteem can be affected by experiences and the people around us when growing up. Childhood experiences, teachers, relationships and significantly, the media, all have a part to play in how we think and feel about ourselves. When you look back on your life, can you remember any points where you or someone else has made you feel 'not good enough'. As children, if a *'not good enough'* message is reinforced often enough by yourself or others, then this sticks and impacts your self-esteem and becomes a limiting belief of the future. Low self-esteem has so many negative impacts on the body and the brain, and stress and repetitive thinking and feeling low can manifest into poor mental health.

Even if you have high self-esteem, we can still have low self-belief. This may be due to one area of your life/past where you have lacked belief in yourself. Low self-belief can present itself as shyness, communication difficulties, social anxiety and lack of assertiveness.

Low self-belief can also cause you to have a strong critical *'inner voice'*. Some call it your inner-bitch, mind-monkey, inner-devil. I didn't have low self-esteem as a child, but also there have been elements in my life that that have caused low self-esteem and in turn a lack of self-belief. Not anymore.

I want you to know that I don't have all the answers. Sadly, this is not the *'answer'*, but it is real. Throughout this whole writing process, I have battled my inner voice, at times being debilitated by the fear that I am not good enough and that nobody would care about reading my book.

I want you to know that every day is a battle for me with my inner voice, my past limiting beliefs and I am still trying to work out what my *authentic self* is, after years of people pleasing. Here are some tips that continue to help me:

Write a list of all the things that you are good at. This may be completely unrelated to your business. Think about something that you know that you are good at – drawing, cooking, singing, puzzles. Think of all the ways that you have mastery in this skill, what successes can you show? Now think about this. Did this skill happen instantly? Were you automatically able to do it or did you have to work on it? Have there been any setbacks? Did you carry on regardless?

I'm going to guess that the answer is *Yes* and that even if you don't shout about your skill, deep down you know you are good and have a belief in yourself.

Let's use the example of painting. If you are good at art, I'm guessing that your primary school drawings were still stickmen and rainbows (seriously I have hundreds of these on my fridge at the minute). You will have honed your skill during school and art classes to become a fabulous artist. You kept going because you believed. Okay, so you may not be an artist, but the example applies to every part of life. We need to believe in our talents and abilities otherwise we won't fulfil our desires.

Are your desires fulfilled? If they are not, then now is the time to say, *'I want more.' 'I believe I am worthy of more'. 'I believe I can have more!'*.

*'Limiting beliefs'* are often spoken about in this entrepreneurial space. Until I came into this space, I wasn't aware of this or the term imposter syndrome. I had been living with limiting beliefs without realising. Limiting beliefs that show up as 'imposter syndrome' and our 'inner critic' all link back to our self-esteem and inner child.

What we need to do with these beliefs is to reframe them. They aren't facts, they are thoughts influenced by belief systems that we have acquired and if you repeat the same limiting belief enough times, you will believe it to be true. You have to reframe the thought and repeat it over and over until you reprogramme that negative belief.

Some of my limiting beliefs were – *I am not a qualified coach.* Reframe – *I am a qualified teacher and these skills are transferable to all parts of life.*

*No one will want to hear my story.* Reframe – *the right people will hear my story and it will resonate with them.*

*People will think I am crazy for giving up teaching.* Reframe – I do not need other people's validation to make choices in my own life.

Have a go yourself. Write down three limiting beliefs that you tell yourself about yourself and then spin it on its head with a reframe.

## Self-awareness & Childhood

There is a lot of research out there looking at the impact of adversity in childhood leaving what is known as Mother and Father wounds. Child abuse and neglect, drug, and alcohol abuse have a huge impact on children. These wounds, which are often left unhealed or buried, can present in adulthood and often transcend the generations, continuing the cycle of damaged and wounded children and adults.

The more I read and learn about co-dependency, I can't help but analyse my own childhood. Childhood wounds are something that I had never heard of until recently and they are so important to understand as they shine a light on our past and help to pinpoint the reason for many triggers. We associate these wounds with a *bad* childhood. It makes sense. But what if you had a *good* upbringing? Can you still have a wound?

I had a lovely childhood, it was abundant with love, opportunity and experiences. We travelled extensively, had a beautiful home, had fun and laughter and still are a very close family. My parents gave me the most wonderful upbringing, guidance, and support, but despite this safe haven and happy life, there was a monster lurking. One that was so unpredictable and so vicious that I often couldn't escape it. I tried my best to keep the monster placated and happy, but it would show up and be triggered by other things - bullies, friends, arguments. That anxiety that lived with me as a child, due to so many things, was insidious at times. Fear of being singled out at school, being left out, friends falling out with me and at home, the fear that my parents were going to split up. When they argued, the monster would rise and I felt that I needed to be good and to not get into trouble for fear of upsetting them, for fear of causing an argument.

From the age of sixteen, I became acutely aware that there were problems in my parent's marriage. I won't go into details as they are not relevant to this book, but with all my knowledge now of the para-sympathetic system and the workings of the trauma system, I know that I lived in fawn for many years. I would often tread on eggshells and try to prevent any blow ups as I was terrified that they would get divorced. However, that didn't mean that I just kept quiet, and I had my fair share of ding dongs where I was grounded, made to sweat for weeks! Trying to be good and have my own opinions was hard, but I respected my parents (and was terrified of them) so I towed the line and generally, we got along brilliantly.

Being aware of their marital problems affected us all. At parties there was always the fear that something would kick off and often it did. Even now at the age of forty-two I get that same, oh so familiar lurch when they are together, and I can sense the mood turning sour. My twenty-first was marred with an almighty kick-off and even now, if I look at the photos, all I can remember is that feeling in my stomach and how upset I was. Thankfully they are friends now and we have a great family relationship.

At sixteen, my worst fear was them getting divorced and not being able to see my dad. I used to cry about it, and I can remember being on a school trip once. on the coach, imagining going to visit Dad at his *'apartment'*, like you see in the films. Little did I know that around this time, Dad had packed his case to leave. I can remember the day so vividly.

Something happened that day. I came home from school and just couldn't keep the cry in. I remember thinking it was strange that Dad was home so early in the day. They were both standing in the hall looking sheepish when I walked in.

I couldn't hold the cry anymore and out it came. I told them what had happened and as the words came out the relief to be telling them was so immense. A boy who had terrorised me since primary school had spread a rumour that I, *'Had sex with my dad.'* I can still remember the horror I felt when he asked me this in science in front of the class with the implication of *'rape'*. It was horrific. I was clever, strong minded and confident and that has to be one of the lowest points for me at school. That same boy had punched me in the stomach at primary school and had made my life a misery. I never stood up to him. At primary school I never stood up for myself, but by the time I got to Fifth Year (in old money, Y11 as it is now) I was well versed in standing up for myself with girls as I'd had so much grief off so many of them. But with the boys it was different. I was never friends with boys and throughout school had always been picked on by this boy, and a few others, for being a *Swot* and a *Snob* because we lived in a nice house. The boys had a huge impact on my confidence, and I never felt that I was fancied by any boys either and so this began my narrative that I was not fanciable.

I just couldn't stand up to that particular boy. Looking back, the arguing and shouting that I witnessed at home made me want to avoid any conflict and thus began the people pleasing and what would lead on to be co-dependency. In my subconscious desire to not be aggressive and angry, I started to pave the way for relationships of the future where I would fawn and please them. I could hold my own in an argument, but I would often tread on eggshells to keep the peace. I would live for many years with that same feeling in my gut that I lived with for the next eight years as my parent's battled on to save their marriage for the sake of the kids.

I don't blame them. They did what they thought was best at the time. Back then divorce was not so common and the stigma of coming from a broken home was apparent. My mum had also suffered the pains of her own parents divorce and I know how much they wanted to keep our family together. It was the best of times and the worst of times towards the end. I have the most wonderful memories and we are all so close now. But as I now know as an adult, staying together for the sake of the kids only hurts you more.

Without even knowing, I was the reason they stayed together. That day when I came home Dad was about to leave. Instead, he sneaked his suitcase back in, they put on a united front to support me at school and were the best parents as they always were. Sadly, this united front meant that the inevitable break up became more bitter and when they eventually separated when I was twenty-four, it still rocked my core and took away that family unit. I'm not sure I have ever really got over it and I don't know if I will.

This isn't their fault - as the saying goes – *'it is what it is'* – they too will both have been affected by their parents' relationships and my mum in particular, when her parents divorced, when I was a baby. My grandad always used to say he had cursed the family and to a point, I think he was right. His betrayal of my grandma shattered my mum's world and the ricochet crept into her marriage, which ended with betrayal, and subsequently, into both mine and my sister's marriages too.

My sister and I have been co-dependents and people-pleasers in our significant relationships, and it is only now, in my forties, post abuse, that I am becoming more self-aware and beginning to piece together the journey that I have been on. Looking through a trauma informed lens has allowed me to be able to have empathy for the pain and trauma that both my parents were experiencing, how they were doing their best for the family, and I can hope to be able to use this new understanding to help others in overcoming their traumas too.

## Healing your inner child

Look back at your life and identify the significant things that have happened *for* you as a child. This is an activity that I did early on and at the time I was unsure as to what it meant. Working out where and how we may have lost some parts of our authentic 'self' can be tricky. Deep within us are the memories of the experiences we had as children. These memories continue to affect our lives in the present and healing begins with the act of reconnecting with your childhood. One way to do this is to feel the feelings you had as a child.

Think about yourself as a little girl. What did you dream of? How does she feel? What were your hopes? What does she enjoy doing? The process of writing this book has taken me back to my inner child and through journaling and writing, discovering your inner child is something that I would encourage you to do.

Healing your wounded inner child can help to improve your sense of self and therefore your self-esteem and self-belief. Our limiting beliefs, low self-worth, negative self-esteem and self-belief are more often than not rooted in our childhoods, and this is a generational cycle. I know that our parents and their parents all did their absolute best for us with the means and love that they could give. Many people sadly do not have the same safety and nurture as others at home and, for as long as domestic abuse, narcissism, drug and alcohol abuse live on in family lives, the cycles will perpetuate. The more the cycle of hurt inner children continues, the more the limiting beliefs and self-sabotage of future adults is manifested.

This isn't about blame, this is about moving on, healing and helping our future generations to not follow the same cycles. We are the cycle-breakers, the healers and the time is now, otherwise this cycle will go on. I will not allow my daughter to suffer from her childhood wounds and by introducing mindfulness and visualisation at such a young age, we are finding ways to address her anger, to alleviate her sense of blame and to give her the vocabulary and ability to articulate her emotions to have a strong sense of self. If only this could be given to every child.

# Chapter 2
# Positivity

*"I am not what happened to me. I am what I choose to become."*

Glass half full or half empty? Who cares just get me another drink... this was a quotation shared on social media from comedian, Sean Locke, who died in 2021. This made me laugh, but it also got me thinking. We often think about whether we are pessimist or optimist but is it as clear cut as that? For many years, I had a negative mindset yet still, deep down, I always hoped for more. This is where adversity upsets the balance of *half-full v half-empty* as sometimes, when faced with adversity, the knock-on effect can be significant.

We've all heard the sayings, *'Thriving not Surviving'* or *'What doesn't kill you makes you stronger.'*

There are memes, sayings or clichés that we see shared all the time. One of my favourites is *'One day your story will become someone else's survival guide*' When you are in the midst of your own story, it can be very hard to see any sort of light; survival is all you have. When you are in your cloud and fog of depression, wanting the world to fade away, it is inconceivable to think that one day you could be someone else's survival guide.

Traumatic, painful, significant events can often dim your positivity but if you want to be more, you have to dig deep and find the positive, despite the negativities in life, practise gratitude and bloody well smile!

Ironically, in order to focus on 'positivity', our attentions lie heavily on adversity and negativity. I am a positive person and positive mindset is the key to my transformation and one that I know will do the same for you. I wasn't like this for a very long time. I am what you might call a recovering pessimist, I never knew that I was a pessimist but I can look back now with a totally different view of my life. The negativity that lived within me, that I can see now linked back to my limiting beliefs and wrongly formed opinion of myself, went on to become self-sabotage and catastrophic people-pleasing attributes, resulting in my timeline of progressively more abusive relationships.

Having a positive mindset seems so simple - the concept being that our thoughts control our belief and actions and so 'like attracts like'. So, by focusing on a positive thought, you will attract more positivity. Think about when you walk down the street, do you smile at people? If someone smiles at you it is very hard not to smile back. If you wake up late, and this has a knock-on effect on your day, the negativity follows you. Now for anyone that knows me, I am certainly not going to lecture you on the importance of getting up early to start the day right! I am still always late, but I do not let that set backs in the morning negatively impact my mood by using positive language and praise with Emilie.

The baggage that we all carry is immense and carrying that shit around is bloody heavy. Sometimes we just want to go to our own pity parties and sit eating all the food, sharing all the memes about whose life is shitter than whose. Or some of us might be living the polished, 'Insta perfect' life, not daring to share the weight and pain that you are living with. I know women who have been through the most horrific of circumstances and cannot or will not share their pain or story. Everyone deals with their baggage differently but what we all must know is that everyone has some.

There is a standing joke with my friends that I always have a story to tell, there's always a drama in my life when theirs are pretty dull. I used to wish for a dull life, to not have these adversities to share but I was wrong. I don't believe that these women had pain free lives, simple, dull or permanently perfect lives. The difference is that I have always been a talker, an over-sharer and if I am honest, a good storyteller that can hold a crowd. My stories have become infamous over the years but when the pain was at its worst, when I needed to reach out to people the most, I stopped sharing. Part of me wanted to write on Facebook, 'I've been strangled, how are you all going on with your lives.' I wanted to shout at people 'He nearly killed me. I don't give a shit' but of course, I didn't.

So, I ask you... what do you carry? What is in your baggage? Emotional abuse, neglect as a child? Narcissistic parents, narcissistic abuse, domestic abuse, chronic pain, depression, divorce, debt, cancer, bereavement, child loss, parent loss... the list really is endless and I know that if you have survived these, at times you will have wanted to cry and scream, you may also have wanted to drift away into the blackness. I also know that if you are reading this, you are *'thriving not surviving'* and your story will help someone else, even if you don't know it yet.

## The Big Five

For years I fixated on achieving the *'Big Five.'* I would often talk about accomplishing them all - but sadly, more often than not, I was missing one or two. There were five things that I wanted in life. Family/Friends, Home, Career, Health and Relationship (aka the 2.4 family) and I always had so much to be grateful for, yet for many years I focused on the negativity of what I didn't have, rather than allowing myself to feel gratitude for what I did have. Positivity doesn't mean that everything has to be sunshine and flowers all the time. Equally, living through adversity doesn't mean that you should wrap yourself up in a blanket of self-pity. We need to find the middle ground.

My *'Big Five'* was always a stick that I used to beat myself with, an impossible false perfection that could never be sustained. This so-called *'Big Five'* was forever changeable and although I always had three safely ticked off, it was health and relationship that were elusive and the ones that caused me the most pain, anxiety and depression. The gratitude that I now have makes me wish that I could go back to Louisa in her late-twenties and thirties and tell her to find the positive and be truly grateful for it. It is true *'What doesn't kill you makes you stronger'* so let me take you through my journey to find the *'Big Five'* and the lessons that I have learned along the way.

At seventeen I met my first 'serious' boyfriend, who I was with for seven years. We grew up together. He was my first love and a great love that will never leave my heart. I was settled down before my time and had missed out on the crazy twenties. I had never worried about meeting 'the one'. I wasn't desperate to get married, I wanted to go to university, to work in television, to write, to act. Those years that I was safely in a relationship blinded me to the possible difficulty of the search for my Mr Right and looking back, I have no clue as to whether I knew my authentic self or not. Without realising it, I was safely on my way to the 2.4 life that, at that point, I didn't even want.

After seven years, we broke up, and my runaway to Majorca and then Australia began my search of my true self, but with this came seven years single and my *'Big Five'* blown apart.

My late twenties were the *'Hey day'* of my partying, travelling, and dating, aka the *'Sex and the City'* days. Or more realistically, the *'Occasional Sex in the Town'* days, (not quite Manhattan) and there was no sign of Mr Big, more Mr Dickhead - and there were plenty of them!

I had a great support network of family and friends from all corners of my life. School, university and work. I had a lovely home - a mortgage and a trendy modern apartment. It was mine and I loved it. The best thing about this time was finding Emma – my lobster. She is the *Samantha to my Carrie,* and we had many a drunken night with the didgeridoo, musical sticks and occasional naked dancing.

Those years were the best years in so many ways, filled with, fun, friends and frivolity. But they were also so lonely. I spent six single Christmases, went to umpteen weddings, christenings and thirtieths alone. All of my school and university friends were *'settling down'* yet I had slid right down my single snake and was very much back at square one. I couldn't have coped alone without by TV friends - SATC was my therapy, Gilmore Girls helped my loneliness and Desperate Housewives was my escapism. Not forgetting of course, continual re-runs of Friends!

Job wise, I was on the up and up. After three successful years in my *'accidental travel career'* I decided that I needed to get back on track. The job that started off running alongside my MA turned into an inadvertent successful sales career taking me through various promotions in the UK and overseas, working as Team Leader, in Recruitment and Training and also part of the Management team to start up a bespoke Long-haul Travel Agency in Liverpool. It didn't light me up. I needed to get find my spark, so I began training to be a teacher.

I retrained as an English teacher, whilst paying a solo mortgage and I was promoted in my second year of teaching to Head of Year and paved a very successful career. This early promotion sent shockwaves around the school as I was regarded as, *'a new teacher, fresh out of college.'* When in fact I had been leading sales teams, managing performance and responsible for problem solving, accountability and motivation in two high profile travel companies. I was far from inexperienced, and my drive has never stopped since.

So, there was always a massive tick next to the career box! I never wanted a baby young and always wanted to *'do well'* in my career, and so striving to achieve in teaching was where most of my energies lay. I was a Head of Year for seven years, moving onto a Leadership and Head of Department position and after having Emilie other leadership roles across the school. Looking back now, I can see that I was in a constant state of *Fight*. I was fighting for recognition and external validation within my role, to keep that people-pleaser part of me happy.

## How's your back?

At the age of twenty-three, I slipped a disc in my lower back. Although I recovered after about six months, this was the beginning of eight years of back problems. From 2002 - 2010 I was plagued with chronic pain. I slipped the disc countless times - every which way possible – by this point I was teaching and had months off sick and treatments that involved keyhole surgery, an invasive epidural, and ultimately major surgery to replace two discs in my spine.

It's to safe to say that my bad back defined my life. People still ask me how my back is, as it was the epitome of who I was for those eight years. I had very little positivity in my life at this time and after the first slip, it came back with a vengeance in 2006 and those subsequent four years were the worst.

At times, it felt that I would never break the shackles of the pain that gripped me twenty-four hours a day.

Pain. It's a bastard. It's also invisible and it is so hard to live an invisible illness. From screaming with agony on the commute to work, spraying deep heat continually, blowing up heat packs in the microwave as I couldn't get them hot enough to take the pain away.

I was waking paralysed with pain on a daily basis, having to wake two hours before I was due to get up to take pain killers that allowed me to live some sort of a life. But the painkillers were numbing my senses and as the pain increased, my dependency on them increased too.

The time I took off sick from work caused so much additional pain too. The stress and worry of work, the paranoia and guilt from being off. The denial until I was at the point where I couldn't stand up, to the acceptance that I had to give in and rest.

There were days where I couldn't bend down to put clothes in the washing machine, times that I couldn't get off the sofa and used the didgeridoo as a walking stick. One morning, I was so paralysed with pain, I couldn't move and I had to take painkillers with cold tea. I can't even count the times I cried with pain, frustration and despair.

These are the invisible moments.

I lived an invisible existence. Everyone knew I was in pain, but no-one knew. No-one knew until someone did... and then he took advantage of my vulnerability.

## I want the Fairy-tale

'*I want the Fairy-tale*' Remember that line from '*Pretty Woman*'? Yes, we've all been there and I expect that, with the media and societal influences that we grow up with, most woman do want just that. The *Cinderella, Glass Slipper, Happy Ending...* roll credits. '*Big mistake... huge.*' Another Pretty Woman line and one of my all-time favourites... and wanting the Fairy-tale, for me, was a *huge* mistake.

My knight in shining armour may as well have ridden in on a white horse as he fully fit the Prince Charming role... and he could cook... double bonus!

But like any Fairy-tale, there is always a bad guy and unfortunately, I married him. The hero became very much the villain of the piece, ripping my *Happy Ever After* cruelly from me with years of debt and trauma as a bonus.

My self-esteem was at an all-time low. I was emotionally and physically vulnerable and although I do not know the facts, I do believe that he 'sought me out' somehow. The coincidences of our meeting, having the same surgeon, same disc problems and finding someone that understood my pain is now, looking back, too coincidental. But that's how it was. *It was meant to be* or so I told myself. What I thought to be him showering me with love and affection was love-bombing, very early manipulation and gas-lighting. I can remember him not going home one day when I was off to work... we'd only been together a week and he made me feel that I was the crazy one for not trusting him to stay at my house.

I came home to a lovely meal, a very tidy house and a candle lit bath and after that, he never left. Within two weeks he had moved in. I was oblivious to this decision and if I questioned it, I was the one made to seem crazy. I was distracted by a grand gesture and so it continued. The people-pleaser in me didn't want to upset the apple cart as finally I had found my Mr Big. *Big mistake. Huge!*

## Ignoring the Red Flags

What is very hard to admit, to myself firstly, and then publicly, is that I have been a victim of not one, but two narcissistic abusive relationships. I married the perfect man who turned out to be a nightmare. He was leading a double life from before we were married and somehow managed to lie and twist everything. I had him on a pedestal and to the outward world, he was the perfect man.

Those limiting beliefs were tapping away at me and my need to be loved and need for external validation was so strong that it allowed me to become blind to the red flags. I wanted to love and be loved in return. The problem was, I hadn't understood how to love myself and I didn't until very recently.

I married a man for all of the right reasons: for stability, for a home, to have 2.4 children and to grow old together. I wanted the picture-perfect house, husband and children... but what I now know is that no matter how good you are at imagining things, if you choose badly, the dream soon becomes a nightmare.

And it did.

He seemed too good to be true. He was. He tapped into my weakness, my insecurities and manipulated them... offering me my hopes and desires. He used my trust and belief in people against me. He took what he wanted and lied his way into my life, into my heart and into my trust.

Eventually his lies caught up with him. I'd been financially and emotionally abused, lied to, manipulated and sold a dream that did not exist.

Through the help of a counsellor, I was able to see through his lies. Told to 'stop doing and to sit back and watch my own life,' I began to notice things. One lie appeared... then another appeared and then it snowballed and I was living a soap opera type life. The life I knew vanished.

He had another partner, his jobs had been fake, money was missing and I was left with many reasons to leave.

But I couldn't leave.

He twisted everything. For every lie he had a plausible reason, he was so desperate to prove that he loved me. It all made sense. I was wrong. None of it was real.

When I was away from him talking to other people I could see the lies, but as soon as I was with him the fog descended and I couldn't think for myself. He would hold my hands and stare so intently into my eyes and his sincere declarations of love and how much he needed me put me back under his spell.

The day that the dream slipped will forever remain in my memory. It hurt; it was beyond painful. But I didn't cry for him. I cried for a marriage, a promise, a life. I cried for the babies that we hadn't had and the family that would never be.

I couldn't believe that this was my life. I packed and moved to my mum's. It had taken three months for me to finally have the courage to leave. Then the suicide calls came. The messages and desperate calls and emails but soon after I was discarded as he moved on in life as quickly as he had arrived.

So, there I was. Thirty-three divorced, childless and alone. It seemed that all of my friends were married, settled down and had been having children for years. I was Aunty and Godmother to several of my friends' children. I loved spending time with them, but that gnaw in my stomach was always there.

Yes, I was doing well in my career, but this was never a Career v Motherhood choice. I never chose to not have a baby, I just never found myself in the right relationship with the right person at the right time. I wanted a baby but I wanted to do things the right way round. Why? I don't know. But there was that instilled sense of tradition of what was right, and so engagement, marriage and baby was the order that things had to be done. How many times did I lie in bed and mentally count out... 'so if I met someone now... we'd need to be engaged by blah and married by blah so that I can have a baby by blah'... I have driven myself mad.

Where does this expectation come from? Why do we, as women, put this pressure on ourselves? Do we blame the Disney *Happy Ever Afters*? The media? Or just generational expectations? The stereotype of the 1950s housewife dates back to the post-war period when England was wanting to put on a show to prove that the economy was strong and we were affluent. The 'woman at home' allowed the man to provide for the family and thus began the stereotypes. Women were the caregivers and their roles, like teacher, nurse, cleaner, centred around care and service rather than profit, allowing the patriarchy to thrive with men in the deemed superior jobs. These masculine and feminine archetypes still exist and such is the battle for equality. Yes, there has been a jump forward, but generations of women before us have fit into the prescribed gender roles and it really is time to Stop Ironing and Start Living, in more ways than one!

As I emerged from the chrysalis of my broken marriage, I realised the mental abuse that I had been living with. The confidence that I had lost. My counsellor was guiding me to find myself, to work on my self-esteem and to love myself first, but sadly, back then I thought I knew best. My broken pieces couldn't be fixed by myself alone. I needed someone else to pick up the pieces, to fix me and tell me that everything would be okay. I craved the rush of love, being with someone and the still overwhelming desire to finally find the perfect 2.4 life, learn from my mistake and find someone totally different.

He was. He was the polar opposite to my ex-husband. But what was glaringly the same was my vulnerability, my low self-worth and the people pleaser in me who was desperate to fix someone else too. We were the perfect match. I had found the validation that I still needed and to heal the wounds that were still open, I plastered them with this new love story.

Things happen for a reason? Right time and place? Or just good luck? Whatever the reason, it worked and for a long time, I thought that I was happy. I was back on track and finally found the perfect 2.4 family - he had a son; we had a baby. We were Facebook happy. It was perfect and I didn't want to lose it all again. But I was ignoring red flags. From just two months in there were signs. He discarded me after Christmas for several days, after months of love-bombing and movie-style romance. I didn't know what I had done wrong. He had introduced me to his son and his family, we had had a magical Christmas together. I couldn't understand why he was cutting me off and I was made to feel desperate to prove my love to him, tested and ignored. I passed the test. I was back in his arms and that sealed my fate for the next six years.

## I Was Only Strangled Once

For a long time, I felt that my domestic abuse wasn't as bad as others. I was a fraud... I mean how can my experience be inspiring if I was only strangled once? I wasn't beaten, I didn't live a horrible life. I was independent and had a good social life. But I was so unhappy.

Of course, my experience was *bad enough* because nobody should ever live in a way where they are emotionally, verbally, physically or sexually abused. Yet I put up with the emotional and verbal abuse and didn't openly question that it was abuse. If I am honest, I did. In both relationships I googled *'What is domestic abuse'*, but I was always able to convince myself otherwise. If you ever have to Google your partner's actions... take that red flag and run!

## Cycle of Abuse

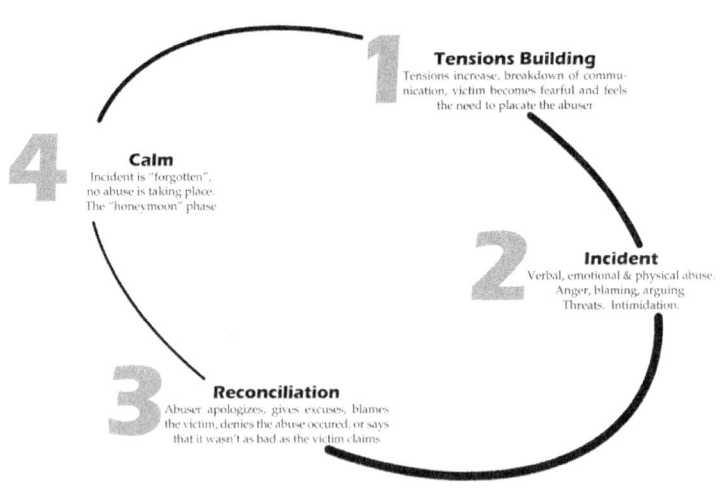

**1. Tensions Building**
Tensions increase, breakdown of communication, victim becomes fearful and feels the need to placate the abuser

**2. Incident**
Verbal, emotional & physical abuse. Anger, blaming, arguing. Threats. Intimidation.

**3. Reconciliation**
Abuser apologizes, gives excuses, blames the victim, denies the abuse occured, or says that it wasn't as bad as the victim claims

**4. Calm**
Incident is "forgotten", no abuse is taking place. The "honeymoon" phase

We lived in a cycle of abuse for six years, but the problem was, I didn't realise fully that this was what it was. I used to describe my life as being 'Stuck in a circle' when talking to friends and now, having done the research, I can clearly pin-point the different stages of the cycle and many times I told friends and family about how I felt trapped in this circle. I knew it had to break, I knew for a long time, long before I had our baby that this cycle needed to break, but Stage three was so powerful and the reconciliation was so good that the Honeymoon Stage 4 would refuel me with the future faking and false hope that it would all be okay and then, without me even realising, we were back at Stage 1, treading on eggshells, the swell before the tsunami of Stage 2.

The cycles became more severe over time and in quicker succession. Even when I broke away and we lived apart, trying to co-parent kept me trapped in this same cycle until ultimately, the escalation of his abuse hit an extreme level and he attacked me.

I have previously written about the day I was assaulted and the subsequent ten months which resulted in my emotional and psychological burnout... unofficially known as *'the breakdown'*. Looking back now, a year further on in my healing, I can see that I was still very much writing from the wound rather than the scar. Just writing the words made me feel panicked and breathless, but I had this urge to share and tell everyone what had happened to me. This comes with further trigger warnings as I will share some of my story; if you are living a life somewhat similar then please stop, look at your life and make a plan.

I left him two years before the assault. Made myself homeless for two months in order to be free of him and to keep us safe. With my then two-year-old, I was living out of my car between family member's houses as I tried to find us a safe home. I moved towns, jobs and started a new empowered life – or so I thought. At that point I knew the relationship was wrong and that I was sad more than I was happy – but narcissistic abuse was not a term that I knew anything about. After a mere two months alone in my new world, I was dragged back into his web and this time, I was caught even more tightly.

What happened is something that I have never spoken of until now. I didn't know if I even had the courage to write about it. In the four months from leaving him I had been bombarded with messages, calls and declarations of love. I can see now that he used the narcissistic traits – love bombing, gaslighting and future faking and as an expert at knowing my weaknesses, he used them to his full advantage. Offering me a new and improved version of him and the life with him that I loved and so wanted to believe could be true. But I was so much happier away from him. I had re-joined my old theatre group, changed jobs and was back home, close to my family.

His coercive control was hard to battle. Over time gaslighting creates the effects of confusion, brain fog, self-doubt, paranoia and you can feel like you are losing your mind. I would question myself, second-guessing what I wanted and who I actually was. The fog would descend when I was with him and inside, I would be screaming at myself to get away from him but his omnipresent stature and belligerent manner meant that even though I didn't feel afraid of him, I was inwardly terrified as I had already experienced violent outbursts from him.

I was so much happier away from him, but I just didn't have the strength to keep telling him over and over again. He would cry and beg me. My self-esteem diminished again and I didn't feel good enough. This self-doubt meant that slowly I was drawn back into his web, I needed him to feel good.

He twisted my thoughts to make me believe that I did want him and that was when he ensnared me. Flirty texts, sexual innuendo and *playful* suggestions had begun to come through. That evening when he dropped the baby off after his weekend, he wouldn't leave. He was still there. After I had put her to bed, he followed me to my bedroom. I can't remember if I asked him to leave. He was kind and funny, the man I loved. I wanted him to leave. I didn't want him there. But the kisses were familiar and safe and filled the aching void in my heart. Did he pressure me? At the time I would have said *No*. I fully participated, and the love and passion were real. But I hadn't wanted it to happen. He had manipulated his way back into my bed; I didn't want to be back with him and suddenly I was.

In a cruel twist of chance, I found out that I was pregnant. Fate sealed. We were back together and then came the task of telling my friends and family, who had helped me to escape him the first time. I felt an urge to tell everyone that I was pregnant in a way to justify my choice. But it didn't feel right. I had put my mask back on and was masquerading life again.

I went away with my Mum to a caravan in Wales. When I was away from him, I could think straight again. I have never spoken publicly about this and I know that there will be divided opinion. I knew deep down that I couldn't bring a baby into such a volatile, abusive relationship. I didn't want to be with him, for mine and Emilie's sake, but I felt shackled to him. At the same time, I had been to see my back surgeon and following the chronic difficulties with my first pregnancy, I was told that there was a very high risk of chronic pelvic girdle pain from early on in the pregnancy and a high risk that it wouldn't go away after birth and I could be wheelchair bound. I was a single mum, with rent to pay, a new teaching job and a two-year-old. There was only one answer.

I made the decision that I would never wish on anyone. The decision that I had feared ever having to make. I told him and despite his declarations of support, his mask began to slip. He wouldn't allow me to bring my mum and on the night of the termination he emotionally tormented me. He left me alone and mocked me for being upset, for asking for his support and I was consumed with guilt and grief for the life that I couldn't love. I hated him. For the first time, I hated him and how he made me feel. He used the hardest thing I have ever done as a way to emotionally abuse me further.

The pain and grief consumed me and without even making the decision for myself he was back. He was there and for a short time was my saviour. I was back in that same vulnerable pit that I had been when I first met him. The strong, empowered Louisa who had left him to start a new life had disappeared again. He moved in, we went in holiday to celebrate, and I carried on, carrying the pain and smiling through the tears.

Fairly quickly his mask slipped completely, and the old ways resumed. This time it was worse. His abuse had started to impact my daughter too. She had witnessed him verbally and aggressively abusing me. She saw the bruises after he'd shoved me over. I was lying to people about the bruises and that was when I knew. Six months later I was stronger, with a new support network from my new job and finally, I made a full break. He moved out and this time it was for good!

Even though I'd physically broken free from him, I was still very much controlled by him emotionally. He tried to control my life and my belief that my daughter needed to have her father in her life meant that I still continued to excuse and ignore his increasingly more volatile, irregular and controlling behaviour. Every meeting with him sent my anxiety higher and higher. His calls became more frequent, he would pop round unannounced; even let himself into my home when I wasn't there. He still had my key. It took me five months to drum up the courage to ask for the key back. My life was still treading on eggshells, and I just didn't know how to escape from his grip.

He was testing me, checking up on me, and no matter what I said I was always made to feel like the one in the wrong. The night he attacked me started when I tried to hold a boundary.

## Boundaries

Boundaries are one of the most positive things that you can put in place to protect yourself. Let me ask you... do you have your own boundaries in place? This isn't just about abusive relationships. Being able to say *No* is one of the best examples of self-care that I can share with you and one that can be very difficult to do. Have a look at the relationships with the people around you. Do you have healthy boundaries? Are you able to say *No* or do you *go with the flow* to please people? Saying *No* has always been something that I have struggled with, especially when it comes to drinking and nights out! But it is okay to say *No*, especially when it comes to keeping you and your children safe. If you or anyone you know is struggling, please reach out to me or the Domestic Abuse contacts at the back of the book.

The more I protected myself and the more distance I put between us, the more erratic he became as he lost more and more control. It took me a long time to find the strength to put these boundaries in place and in fact, it was friends and family that supported me to, as I didn't have the strength on my own. My friend Roisin from work was the voice of reason and strength that I needed when I struggled to find it on my own as I was so afraid of what might happen if I did.

I could see him beginning to unravel as I found the strength to stand up to him. To make him leave my home when he was being abusive. To refuse to take his calls. All of this resulted in more abuse and bombardment of texts. The day he attacked me was because I had put the phone down on him when he was verbally abusing me the day before. This abuse continued on my drive, in front of our nearly four-year-old. The conversation wasn't going well, I knew that he was not in any position to calm or be placated. The only way to try and diffuse the boiling rage was to walk away and close the door. This enraged him more. By walking away from him and not arguing back I was putting a boundary in place and the more I held onto my boundaries the more irrational his behaviour had become. Trying to shut the door to keep him out of my house is what made him flip.

That was the day when my world spun on its axis. Life as I knew it changed. I had yet again been a victim of narcissistic abuse for six years - emotionally, mentally, verbally and physically. Yet as a strong, educated and confident woman, it took another six months before I could fully say out loud that I was a victim of abuse. I am a victim of abuse.

When the police interviewed me and asked if he'd ever done anything like this before I said *No*. Well, he didn't hit me... so was it abuse? But what about the time he pushed me... grabbed my face... restrained my wrists... threw things at me? Yes, all of this and more. As the Police Officer asked probing questions, six years of abuse unfolded. Verbal abuse – calling me names, swearing at me, mocking me. Mental abuse... always making me believe things were my fault, twisting the truth, lying. Turns out he was quite the expert.

He was charged and pleaded guilty to *Assault with battery*, which, in a recent law change could have been *Non-fatal Strangulation*, and family court found twelve cases of *Physical, Emotional and Verbal Abuse* to be *Fact*. I filed for a non-molestation and non-contact order which were granted. The first time I faced him was a week after. Face to face in court. Our names tagged against each other. *War of the Roses.* He couldn't look at me. My stomach was in knots but I stared at him. He caught my eye – I stared until he looked away. I was strong and defiant on the outside but inside, it was another story.

In the previous two years of trying to break free of him, my anxiety and depression worsened. Medication was increased steadily and the aftermath of the attack is a blur. The assault was June 2019. I took nine days off work and then tried to get back to normal. Overnight, I was a 24/7 single mummy with no shared contact and a very stressful, pressured, full-time teaching job, with additional responsibilities and a looming OFSTED inspection. My GP warned me that if I didn't deal with *it,* things could get worse. I didn't have a clue how to deal with *it,* so I made myself very busy having a lovely life and cracked on with work.

My toxic positivity took over and I began running the *Mummy is Fine show.* Do you find yourself immersed in toxic positivity sometimes? That fear of not being able to complain about your crappy place in life as *At least you've got your health,* or, *other people have it so much worse than you.* The feeling that you have to just put on a smile and carry on as everyone is too busy and so you just get on with it! In photos I smiled, we laughed and I went on holidays, nights out and even dated. But behind the positive smile, there was a darkness in my eyes and demons in my head that weren't being dealt with.

Sixth months later, two court appearances, OFSTED, Scarlett Fever and many other stresses, I broke down. It was December, I was done. I could no longer cope with life as a single mummy, full-time English teacher and an ongoing court case. My little one was also struggling with anxiety, nightmares, loss of her dad.

I was mentally broken. How do you tell people how broken you are when on the outside, you are smiling and confident? Every day I was faking life in work, with my friends. The dark fog was getting darker and the new enemy, anxiety, had taken over. Everyone knew I'd been assaulted and it was no longer spoken about, but it was all I could think about. Every waking and sleeping thought I was consumed by it. Sleep was no escape. Nightmares that I cannot even begin to repeat. Too harrowing to dream, let alone to try and remember. But all were linked to the attack; the fear, the anxiety. Even writing this now, I feel like I have a size twelve boot standing on my chest. Tears stinging in my eyes as I try not to go back there. I broke down in tears in a lesson with some lovely pupils. Pupils on the corridor saw me crying in the morning, on my way into class. Hyperventilating in the car as I drove past his house, reliving a nightmare.

Ten months of court hanging over me took its toll and in February 2020 it was over. As I left the courtroom, I only just made it into the toilet before an intense guttural cry escaped my body. The cry reverberated around the old, echoey building. I have never cried like that before or since. Such a gut-wrenching cry of pain, relief, despair and disbelief. One that I hope never to experience again. It was over. I didn't have to face him again and finally, I was able to stop fighting and begin to deal with *it*.

After the intense, all-consuming adrenaline of court and the final result, I was left deflated. A hopeless balloon with no life left. For the next week I was absent. I lay on the sofa for days and nights on end. Trapped in waking sleep and suffocated by my own thoughts. Only getting into some semblance of dress to do the school run. I was broken. *It* had broken me.

Slowly, I began to rebuild my strength and during therapy, I began to take control of my own vision and my own future. After being off work for two months, something had shifted in me. The career driven teacher realised that it was okay to not be a full-time teacher with a responsibility; always striving for the next promotion, to be Outstanding, sending my daughter to breakfast club and afterschool club, spending weekends and evenings marking, hearing my daughter say *'You love marking more than me'*, missing her assemblies, Harvest Festival and class open days.

For twenty years, the career tick on my *'Big Five'* had been consistent but something had shifted. I realised that I could still be career driven, but I could change gear so that the speed of the drive suited the journey that I wanted to be on. I decided that I was going to start my own business. It was whilst sitting in a therapy session that I gave myself permission to be *more*. I realised that nobody was forcing me to be a teacher and that just because I had spent sixteen years of my life teaching, it didn't mean that I had to stick to the plan. I allowed myself to believe that I could be more, do more and ultimately have more. I decided that I was going to turn my adversity into positivity and reignite my spark that had long been forgotten.

I was ready to find my authentic self and in doing so, I have re-ignited my true passion of writing whilst still using my coaching, teaching and leaderships skills.

## Do Things Happen for a Reason?

Do you believe that we are all on a set path? One of my favourite plays is Romeo and Juliet, in particular, the discussions around fate and destiny. Despite the famous line, 'A pair of star-crossed lovers take their life', Shakespeare is thought to have been a believer of free will over fate, which has created many a good debate. Romeo and Juliet is dubbed the 'Greatest Love story of all time' but it is, in fact, a tragedy. And from great adversity comes positivity. It is the deaths of the lovers that mends the 'ancient grudge' of the Montagues and the Capulets and this is the ultimate testament to positivity from adversity!

Fate or free will? I have never quite been sure, but what I do know is that by trusting my instinct and following my gut, I have found my way back to the path that I always was meant to be on. That surfboard was always there, I just had to step back onto it.

The *'Big Five'* doesn't exist and it is no longer something that even comes into my mind. I am grateful for what I have, and I know that I wouldn't be the coach I am now, or the mum, or the writer if I hadn't experienced these adversities.

Everyone I have met on this journey has a story to tell and I hope that by reading mine, I will inspire and empower you to know that you can be, do and have anything you want in the life because the only person you have to back is yourself. You are only gambling with yourself and so it is down to *you* to never let yourself down. And even if you do make a mistake or choose badly; take the lesson and move on!

## Turning Adversity into Positivity

The day that I decided to change my mindset was March 2020... a week before the first national lockdown. I'd been struck another blow not long after being signed off work when I found out, around Christmas time, that my landlord was selling my house. I was still going through the family court process, crippled with anxiety and panic attacks, and supporting Emilie's PTSD and mental health was tough too. So, on top of everything else I was dealing with buying and selling houses. I spent most of the time crying or trying not to cry. Sleep didn't bring any relief as my nightmares were plagued with anxiety and flashbacks. My dreams were at times more horrific than what I'd experienced. I was raped, slashed with knives, and the repetitive nightmare that I was afflicted with the most was being chased and trapped. I was on the run every night, terrified, breathless, searching for Emilie, confronted by him. When you hear the phrase waking up in a hot sweat, it sounds a bit cheesy, but this is what it was like. I would drag myself out of the horror of the dream, catch my breath, only to go straight back to the never-ending torment. As such, my nights got later and later as I avoided sleep.

Waking up from a night of flashback dreams was even harder. The triggers were real and I would wake with the same anxiety and dread as if he were in the room with me. Some mornings the effort needed to get out of bed and take Emilie to school, whilst reliving the horror of the memories and the triggers, was debilitating. This is one reason why lockdown was a blessing for me. We were given the time to heal that we needed. It was bloody hard, don't get me wrong, but the time to stop doing and *Just Be* was the maker of us. I can't remember when the nightmares stopped. It felt like they would be with me forever. I was gripped with them as if I was still living with my tormentor. They still pop up from time to time, but with the skills and healing techniques that I now have, I can separate the reality from the memory, telling myself 'I am safe. This isn't real. This is my brain playing tricks on me'

The day that I attended a Vision Board workshop in a little Gin bar in Lymm was the day that my mindset shifted from negative to positive. I cut out words that held positivity and strength. I sobbed throughout most of the session, I tucked myself away in a booth on my own and focused on my vision. My board wasn't about material gain, it was about my feelings, emotions and taking positive action for my future.

Above all, it included the one thing that I have dreamed of my whole life. My ultimate surfing goal... to be a best-selling author. But to be an author, I would have to start writing again!

I told myself, then and there, that positivity was my new mantra. I left that day knowing that there had been a monumental shift in my thinking, my mindset and in turn, my future. I was going to write and I was going to start my own business.

Positivity was definitely my new mantra.

## Chapter 3
# Affirmations

*"Your mind is a powerful thing. When you fill it with positive thoughts, your life will start to change."*

Do you need help to get past your own limiting beliefs? You may feel stuck in a job, house or relationship that you don't love, but if you don't believe that you are ready and deserving for more then you will stay stuck. Tag me on the socials telling me that you are ready to #SISL – Stop Ironing, Start living! This is exactly what I did.

With my new positive mindset, I set about changing my life. It was time to work on believing *'I am enough'*. Having never even come across an affirmation before, I was feeling a little lost but one thing was for sure, It was time to stop ironing, take down the ironing board, turn it into a surfboard and start living the life that I really wanted. But there the hell did it start?

I had never been aware of universal energy before and I wasn't sure who I was talking to, but I told the universe that I was ready for change, that I wanted more and that night, I was offered free tickets to an event called, *Womanifest*. I will tell you more about this later but it was that initial sign from the universe that made me trust and feel sure that if I asked, believed and put trust in myself, I could receive. All of a sudden, life was a whole lot more exciting.

One of the speakers at *Womanifest* spoke about quitting her job when she was off sick. This was me. I was at that point still signed off and was dreading the return. The Absence review meetings had been conducted in such a horrific manner that they had contributed significantly to my trauma, nightmares and anxiety. After one of the meetings, having felt so attacked, I had a panic attack and collapsed. I was so close to quitting, but that wasn't me. I was an outstanding teacher and I didn't want to leave the profession out of the back door. So, I worked on my mindset starting with affirmations.

This new positive mindset allowed me to begin to reason with my irrational brain a little more and so I began to put a plan into action to start living the life that I really wanted.

I started by healing myself and Emilie.

## Finding the Purple Magic

It is no surprise that the more I struggled with my mental health, the more Emilie did too. When I was signed off work, I was finally able to put myself and Emilie first. I was consumed with guilt as Emilie was struggling so much but at this point, January -

a whole seven months after she witnessed the abusive assault - I hadn't yet been able to put anything in place to support her.

We had been to the GP months before and referred to CAMHS but due to her age, we hit a brick wall. When I was working full-time, the constraints put on us by the school meant that we couldn't take medical leave in school hours, I could never ring the doctors to even get an appointment and the whole thing added to the intense stress that I was under.

I know now that I should have had support from an IDVA (Independent Domestic Violence Advocate) but as I had changed my phone number, I got lost in the system. It was only months later when Emilie had her school Age Four check that I was told about the notes on my file saying that they had tried to contact me. I hadn't received anything by post and had battled on alone.

Once I had the time away from the pressures of school, I was able to take my daughter to the doctors again. The GP was so understanding as I told her about Emilie's nightmares, soiling herself after receiving a letter from her dad. I told her that Emilie's separation anxiety was so bad that she would scream if I went into another room without her, how demanding Emilie was of me and how much emotional strain that was causing. I told her about Emilie hitting herself in the head, pulling her hair and screaming for me to *Take the bad things away*. I was desperate for help, guilty that I had nothing in place and hoping for the answer.

Her reply was, "Sadly there is a gap in the NHS for this age group. If CAMHS won't see you, you could call the NSPCC."

I left feeling defeated, desperate and totally alone.

A few weeks later, after we visited the area where we used to live with her dad, Emilie had the worst episode that I have experienced. It was terrifying for me and beyond distressing for her. As we drove past where we used to live, she recognised things and became angry, "Thanks for putting Daddy back in my head, Mummy!" she spat out at me. We had also arranged a long overdue meet up with her brother, who she desperately wanted to see. It didn't go as planned, Emilie became upset and distant as the afternoon went on. That evening as we drove home, she broke down. We were on the M56 as she cried, screamed, kicked and gave the most guttural cry. She hit herself in the head relentlessly screaming to *Take Daddy out of her head*.

It took several hours to calm her, and her state terrified me so much that I did indeed phone the NSPCC as the Doctor had suggested. The woman that I spoke to was a wonderful support and helped to calm me but she was aghast at the fact that I'd been told to ring. There were no well-being or safeguarding risks and so the ball was firmly back in the GP or School's court.

I vented my frustration on Facebook and my oldest friend from primary school, Clare, reached out to me. She told me about a lady that she'd worked with who was a Relax Kids coach. I wasn't sure what it was but I was desperate for something. When I'd spoken to her on the phone, I felt so at ease. The first session changed my life. Something special happened that day. It was January 2020, seven months after the attack and the class which was supposed to be for my little one helped me to start to heal too.

During the class, there was section where we massaged each other and as we did, I started to cry. Just a few tears. Then an almighty release came. I couldn't understand where it was coming from. I tried to shield the tears, but a knowing smile made me know that I was safe, and it was okay to show my emotion.

After this, it was time to relax. We lay down together on the sofa with lavender filled blankets and we were still. At 12pm on a Saturday, with a four-year-old, I was still. She read two magical visualisations, we lay still and relaxed for twenty minutes! In our chaotic life, filled with anxiety and pain, we had never been so close and still. When the session finished, we both cried together, we clung to each other and sobbed.

It was a release that we both needed. In that moment I knew that Relax Kids was special.

In the following sessions, I learned about the power of affirmations. We would say together *'I am special I am happy. I am Kind. I am Calm.'* It is hard to imagine a life without them now, but back then I didn't talk to myself in a very nice way and so introducing positive ways to believe myself was enlightening.

I started to research Relax Kids and was thrilled to see the franchise opportunities. Sitting in a soft play centre I felt a real buzz of excitement as I read about the company and thought about how this could be the answer that I was looking for. In that moment, I knew that I was going to go for it. My foggy brain couldn't quite work out how it was possible, but I knew that like the phoenix, I had to rise from these ashes and that eventually I could come back stronger.

But sadly, that was still a way off. I had the final court hearing to contend with and that was all consuming. I couldn't sleep with anxiety, but in my insomniac state, the Relax Kids magic kept drawing me back. I must have read the information a thousand times. The escapism and the dream of a chance to work with and support other families like us was very much alive. But it wasn't until I attended that pivotal vision board session that I gave myself permission to go for it!

I arranged several meetings with other business owners that I admired for jumping out of their boring jobs and going for it in a range of businesses. At first, I felt like an imposter as I spoke to them about their businesses, and I was paralysed with imposter syndrome that I could even be contemplating leaving my sixteen-year career in teaching. It was ludicrous. Wasn't it? My friends and family were understandably dubious, but talking to these women gave me spark to know that this is what I wanted. I wanted more.

Spending £1k on a course was well out of my means at that point. It felt huge, and I had never spent such a vast amount on something that was just for me, but I fully believed in the value that it would deliver and the earning potential that came with it. I was also drawn to the purple magic and the positive world that I had stepped into. After the vision board session, and then *Womanifest* and meeting so many inspiring women, I gave myself permission to go for it. I took the first step.

My training was the Saturday 21st March, the day after Boris announced that we would be going into Lockdown on the Monday. I didn't attend the course. I stood and looked at my vision board and sobbed. All this hope and all these visions that I had committed to for 2020 were pulled from beneath me. That old Louisa, the pessimist returned. My inner dialogue reminded me that, of course, something bad had happened to me. And I very nearly listened... but then I looked at the very top line of the vision board. Without even being able to contemplate what could be lying ahead in the next two years of a global pandemic, I had written, *All in Good Time*. This wasn't a race; this was a vision and a journey, not an immediate destination.

Filled with drive, I had my whole future mapped out. I didn't attend and I felt like my world had ended. My dream was over. Lockdown, on top of missing out on the training, sent me spiralling back into depression and anxiety. Coronavirus was taking away all of my plans and significantly, my control. I was also due back at work on a phased return, I had requested part-time but nothing was guaranteed. I felt like the pipe dream had come to an end and I had to return to the rat-race.

During Lockdown, we were both having severe nightmares. My little girl's night terrors were awful. Her attachment to me was so severe and her PTSD meant that she couldn't bear me being alone downstairs. Her teacher had bought her a worry monster. Reading her worries made me weep: *"I worry that my Daddy will hurt Mummy,"* *"A bad man will take Mummy away"*. The bedtime routine had become so stressful that we would both be in tears as she would beg me to *"Take the bad thing away. Make the bad dreams stop. I'm scared of the monsters and daddy."* Affirmations became my go-to to try and support her, 'I am calm, I am safe' being our favourites.

Marneta Viegas and team at Relax Kids HQ designed an online training programme. Whilst waiting to complete the training, I ordered the Relax Kids books and 'had a go' at using the techniques that we'd been taught in our sessions. For weeks, she had cried and screamed in her sleep. The first night that we read the Visualisations, she went to sleep calmly after the second story. A week later and it was still working. We both slept so much better and this is where our recovery began.

I completed the online training but the world had stopped. My ideas of schools, clubs and nurseries to approach was doomed. I was trained but how on earth could I make this business work without any kids? God bless Zoom! It was the saviour of Lockdown in so many ways and enabled me to launch my business from home. Lockdown was the perfect time to launch as the aim of the company is Creating Calm, Confident Children in Chaotic times!

When I saw a plea on Facebook for a Mum looking for ways to support her anxious son, I got in touch. Boom! I had my first PAID one-to-one booking! As soon as these sessions began, I was in my element and planning and delivering *Magical Adventures* for him was the highlight to my week. Then the snowball effect happened and slowly I built up more classes and one-to-ones, all on Zoom. By the end of July, I'd already made half my initial outlay back! I knew that the gamble was worth it and it was paying off financially, but for me, more importantly, it was also paying off mentally and emotionally.

I was beginning to believe it when I said, '*I am happy*' '*I am calm.*'

My mental health was also improving. I had lived in such a negative state of mind for so long and I was representing a company that made work fun and made me feel mentally and physically healthier and happier. I was promoting mindfulness and I was all in with *practise what you preach*. Stretching and simple yoga became a central part of my life and worked almost as a factory reset when I could feel anxiety and panic coming over me.

Together we learned and began to use breathing techniques that now seem so simple, but if no-one teaches you them how do you know? I had never been to yoga (apart from once in NYC when I was trying to be cool and act like a local), I always thought that I was too fat to do yoga. It turns out, I'm pretty flexible for a size 20! The more positivity I gave out, the more Emilie began to calm too. We were healing together.

## Building Affirmations into Your Life

Do you use affirmations? If so, how are they a part of your life? Affirmations have to work for you in a way that feels natural and not forced. Some people advocate looking yourself in the eye in the mirror and repeating the affirmation. I have always found this a bit cheesy. Some people like to stick post-its on their mirror, wall, fridge. For me it was downloading an affirmations app that made the biggest difference. Every day, I am sent affirmations, positive quotations and phrases and they do seem to appear at the most opportune moments.

Only last week, I was talking to my mum about the fact that the court process is beginning again. This time around, I don't crumble at the sight of a brown envelope like last time, but it is still, of course, a little worrying and stressful. Just as I needed it, the message came through, *"You've done it before and you can do it now."*

Another way that I began to use affirmations was when could feel a rise in my chest of anxiety. If I started to become breathless due to a trigger, whispering to myself '*I am safe, I am protected*' often helped me and in the morning, after a nightmare, '*I am safe, this is not real, this is not real.*'

## Don't Believe Everything You Think

Negative self-talk is so common that we largely don't think about how badly we speak to ourselves. Think about any of the negative things you have thought about yourself today: *too fat, too thin, lazy, stupid, bad mum...* it goes on. Changing our self-talk is a huge part of re-affirming your trust, belief and love for yourself. This was what I had to really work on. Having been a people-pleaser and emotionally abused it is hard to re-wire that thinking, but it can be done. I used to think the most negative, awful things about myself but slowly, by affirming myself with positive self-talk, this has improved. I am still a work in progress but I know that if you speak more kindly to yourself, this is the first step to loving yourself and finding even more spark within you.

Build some affirmations into your daily routine and see for yourself. It is a positive way to reframe negative thinking, imposter syndrome and limiting beliefs. These must be written in the present tense and begin with the phrase 'I am, I allow, I choose...' Set a reminder on your phone or download an app and bring some daily belief into your life. Here are some to get you going:

I am safe

I am special

I am strong

I am confident

I am worthy

# Affirmations

I am enough

I welcome change

I am in charge of my choices

I choose calm energy in my life

I allow peaceful thoughts into my mind

I am filled with calm energy and trust in the universe.

# Chapter 4
# Receive

*"What you think you become. What you feel you attract. What you imagine you create."*

— Buddha

The giving and receiving of rings. Do you give to receive? The term *'receive'* is not one that I ever really gave much thought to. Do we always give to receive? Christmas and birthday we receive presents and generally, the consensus is meant to be that the giving is more important than receiving. For any *Friends* fans out there, you will see that I am steering dangerously close to Joey's *'Giving and receiving'* speech, but I do have a point. What are you open to receiving into your life and your business? Are you open to abundance? Eighteen months ago, I didn't understand what abundance even meant and so I am assuming that you might not be fully clear either. If the *Yin* to abundance's *Yang* is *'giving'* then how do we *Give* in order to open ourselves to *Receive* abundance? And what does abundance even mean?

The dictionary definition of Abundance is *a very large quantity of something*. However, in spiritual terms, it is less about having plenty of material objects but revolving instead (once basic needs are met), around *an appreciation of life in its fullness, joy and strength of mind, body and soul*. This is where any non-woo people might start to think *'what the bloody hell is she going on about?'* I was never into spirituality (which I refer to as woo) and in all honesty, thought it was a load of hippy crap. But the meaning of abundance does rely on cultivating respect for the creative energy of the universe. How the heck do we do that?

Before I began to respect the universe, I was consumed with negative thoughts and without much understanding, would openly declare that the universe hated me, yet I wasn't doing anything to show love or respect to the universe. I have always believed in God and some form of fate, but I had never really pinned down what my beliefs actually were.

Are you open to asking and believing that you can receive abundance? I wasn't, and as I already said, I didn't really know what abundance meant. My holistic therapist, Rebecca from *Thyme to Heal*, introduced me to a Meditation challenge for abundance. Every night, I would listen and chant about welcoming abundance into my life yet, deep down at that time, I didn't believe or understand what I was asking for as I hadn't yet opened up to the belief that I was worthy.

There was a pinnacle moment where this began to change. As I lay on the sofa in a vortex of doom day after day, I began to listen to *'The Secret'* and for the first time, I was introduced to *The Law of Attraction*. A few days later I was invited to the vision board session – I didn't know but the universe was already responding.

I reluctantly went along, in all honesty because my mate forced me to and it was a chance to escape the house that had become my prison as I'd been off sick for three months by this point and not getting much better! A local lady, Amy O'Neill, arranged the session and the guest speaker was author and Happiness Mentor, Toni MacKenzie. As I listened to her speak about her triumph over adversity and how the Law of Attraction had changed her life, I sobbed. Every word resonated with me. From within the depths of my anguish and despair, a spark flickered and there was a shift.

I sat in a booth on my own and created my very first vision board. I put my intentions down and they became goals as they became real visions in my future. I left the session a different person and I haven't looked back. *Like attracts like. Positivity attracts positivity.* From there, my *Bad luck* turned to a *Run of luck* and a *Run of Positivity*.

Twelve months later, every vision on my board had become reality.

## The Law of Attraction

Simply put, the *Law of Attraction* is the ability to attract into our lives whatever we are focusing on. It is believed that regardless of age, nationality, or religious belief, we are all susceptible to the laws which govern the universe. The *Law of Attraction* uses the power of the mind to translate whatever is in our thoughts and materialise them into reality. In basic terms, all thoughts turn into things eventually. If you focus on negative doom and gloom you will remain under that cloud. If you focus on positive thoughts and have goals that you aim to achieve, you will find a way to achieve them with massive action.

I have since learned so much more about this from the amazing Niki Kinsella and although I say that *I'm not woo,* I must admit that this central belief shows that I am *a little bit woo, woo curious* or maybe I don't even need a label. All I know is that by opening myself up to a new way of thinking and accepting the possibility of something, an almighty shift occurred and this shift in energy, whether governed by the universe of by my own self, is one that changed the course of my life, my mental health and future career choices.

The Law of Attraction is governed by the concepts: *Ask, Believe, Receive.*

The concept being that our thoughts control our belief and actions, and so 'Like attracts like'. So, by focusing on a positive thought and being very clear and focused on visualising the thought, you can then in turn believe that it can be true and are therefore opening yourself up to receiving. Being open to receive abundance in any form, again comes back to affirmations and reframing your thinking like we are rewiring faulty electrics. Being open to receiving abundance means that you are living in a positive mindset and believe that you are worthy to receive, whether that be an abundance of love, money, happiness. Yes, you guessed it, the reason that I didn't know what abundance meant is because I had lived in a scarcity mindset which linked back to my childhood limiting beliefs.

Think about your own feelings about money, love, happiness, friends, opportunities. Are all of these limitless and open to you? Or do you have a ceiling that prevents you from confidently saying that you can and will receive more? Being intentional with your affirmations can also rework your attitude of abundance and give you a limitless life.

Here are some of the affirmations that you can use to receive more. Pick one and give it a try. How does it feel to say those words and to actively admit that you are ready, deserving and ready for more?

I am worthy of love/money/happiness.

Love/money/happiness flows to me.

I am open to receiving love/money/happiness.

I am entitled to an abundance of love/money/happiness.

## Ignite Your Vision

You already know the power that creating a vision board gave to me and how it became the catalyst to where I am now. Do you have a vision board already? If not, then the next thing you are going to put on your 'to-do list' is to create your vision board. Check out the section at the end on how you can jump onto my session!

A vision board is more than a collage of pictures on a board. It is filled with purpose and is a way to visualise your goals and dreams and be intentional in what you want to receive into your business and your life. It gives you focus and clarity and by centring on your key purpose, can make you way more productive. You can make one the old-school way, with magazine cut-outs, or you can go high tech and use Pinterest.

Your Vision board will help you to *Ask and Believe*. Be specific with what you want to include. Be purposeful about which areas of your life it will focus on. Think about the feelings and abundance that you want to *Receive,* and be specific with what you are open to receiving and are *Asking* the Universe for.

Take a moment to stop reading and imagine yourself in one year's time. I want you to ask yourself:

What do you want to *be*? How do you want to *feel*? What do you want to *have*? These are the fundamental questions to set your intentions for your vision board, whether that be as a woman/mother/partner or in your business?

Let me see your vision boards... tag me in them @mamasignited and use #IGNITEYOURVISION

## Money Mindset

Abundance often makes us think about money. Yes, it is fundamentally about mind, body and soul but I have also come to learn that we should not be afraid or embarrassed to ask for and to welcome an abundance of wealth into our lives. Money doesn't equal success and money doesn't necessarily bring happiness but it is okay to say that you want to achieve more and with that, to earn more and be able to provide more for your family and live life with more freedom and choice.

What is your money story? Have you ever even considered it? For years, I never even put on the lottery, not because I thought it was a waste of money, but honestly because the thought of winning terrified me. Crazy, huh?

Everyone has one and yet it becomes so intrinsically linked to who we are that many people don't even realise that a (usually) negative money story is one of the major blocks in your life.

I was one of those people.

I didn't know that I had a negative money story until I ready Toni Mackenzie's 'Your Flight to Happiness'. It was when I read the book and I did the tasks that she recommended that it hit me like a slap in the face. Once I knew my own money story, I couldn't believe how obvious it was and how I had been oblivious for so long. What did I find out?

My money story basically is that I am afraid of money and with that afraid of success because I associate success with money and having money with bullying, fear and pain, because this is what I grew up experiencing.

I have already shared some of my limiting beliefs that have derived from childhood, and my money story I now know to be own of my biggest wounds from childhood. It began when we moved house. The house that brought my family so much love and joy brought me pain and torment. My parents had worked so hard to afford the house and it was more than a house; it was a wonderful home for many years. But it was also the perfect supply for bullies to feed off and feed they did.

So, now, in my forties and writing my money story, I can see that I have always associated wealth with the bullying and therefore my protector parts and safety system have kept me safe by creating a fear of success, which has shown up as procrastination, self-sabotage and limiting beliefs. That is in the areas of my life where success feels unsafe, and it's not just money. It has appeared in hobbies such as musical theatre, dancing and in relationships. To an extent in my teaching career too.

On the flip side I succeeded greatly in my career and never stopped going for promotions, but it never felt safe. Succeeding always meant that I had to seek external validation, this being something that I have only just learned. Bullying and name calling through my early life meant that I never felt safe to be me, wanted to be someone else and began a lifelong need to be validated for every choice that I made.

All of this links back to money mindset as these fears and limits, in terms of seeking validation, have meant that despite my so-called confidence and outwardly appearing high self-esteem and self-belief, inside I have always been afraid to be the best, to be wealthy, to achieve because in my early development days, all of these things were unsafe. So much so that I never put the lottery on, never gamble because the fear of winning is too much.

Learning this about myself in the last few years has opened my eyes to many other limiting beliefs and I still have to work on having an abundant mindset rather than a scarcity mindset. But now, if I won the lottery, I'd see freedom, safety and choice… so maybe I should start buying a ticket!

## Money Mindset & Financial Abuse

Winning money wasn't the only thing that worried me, spending did too! I would spend generously on holidays and then afterwards need everyone's approval that I'd done the right things. I would stress about the money I'd spent and want to cancel. But it didn't stop me booking the next one! Holidays were my escapism, and the pandemic has made me appreciate not being able to run away and has allowed me to spend my money, energy and worrying on other things... namely this business.

Needless to say, spending £1k on myself would never have happened until this point in my life. Despite the fact that for the whole of my adult life I had had a secure job with a good salary, I was always skint. Not because I am frivolous, but down to the relationships that I was in. Somehow, in every relationship, I ended up being the 'breadwinner' - whether that be down to redundancy, the job market, injury or downright being lied to... every time I seemed to be the one holding everything together. I never needed a man for his money, I have been financially independent since I went to university and paid for my own fees, halls of residence and car. I prided myself in the fact that I left university having not even used my student overdraft! I was so careful with money and so hardworking that I worked every weekend, sometimes two jobs and always full time in the holidays. I paid my way and I was proud of that. This stemmed back to childhood where I had a paper round and proudly saved up for my first pair of Dolcis shoes in my Midland Bank Account. I have always had a good work ethic and understood the value of money.

This didn't last and post university, with the debt of the MA denting my back pocket, I was in the upside-down bank account and didn't see the light of the plus sign for a very long time. This allowed me to re-write my money story that I was *Bad with Money*, but what I was doing was people-pleasing, living beyond my means and pretty much paying for everything in several of my relationships.

I bought my own property age twenty-four, got on the ladder (well and truly putting up that ironing board) but I made good decisions and despite this, still beat myself up about the state of my finances.

Previous boyfriends had egged me on to use the credit card or been a part of my wild *'Let's go on a holiday'* plans but they had never financially abused me. I was in my overdraft, bits and bobs on credit cards, so a few thousand, max. By the time I escaped my abusive marriage I was left £20k in debt with a house that I couldn't sell and another six years of hell trying to get him off the mortgage, despite the fact he, in true narcissist form, had very quickly moved on to his new relationship, aka narcissist supply, and had completely discarded me and the life that we had built together.

The financial abuse was so slight and so manipulative that still, to this day, I find it hard to believe. I didn't want a joint bank account. I said no and was very happy to stay financially independent. I can't fully recount the lies and the manipulation that he used, but he told me that his account had been closed without his permission and he needed an account for his wages. Lo and behold, before I knew it, we were sitting in the bank and I was signing my account over to him. The next week, he lost his job. He lost numerous jobs - so many, I cannot even begin to recount. I was on a good wage as a Head of Year and so we should have been okay on one wage, but somehow, I was always skint. The money would go well before the end of the month. So, we would get things on *Buy now, pay later* - in my name, of course.

His gaslighting and manipulation was so severe and started so early on that I didn't have a chance to realise. Within the first few months of the intense Love-bombing stage, when I was being treated like a queen and was living the fairy-tale that I had been dreaming of, he stole my credit card from my purse, took out cash back and replaced the card. The transaction was on my account in black and white. Yet somehow, I accepted his denials, begs and pleads and incredulous declaration of *How could you think that of me?* So, I apologised. And it so it went on. I was in deep and the financial and emotional abuse continued.

His financial abuse baffles me as he left with what he came into the relationship with. Nothing. We bought a house, got engaged, married and divorced within three years. Those three years ripped so many layers off me that in all honesty, it took until my breakdown of 2020 to begin to deal with them. The debt left me living with guilt and a deep shadow for ten years. The debt haunted me as a constant chain around my ankles pulling me back to that time. The house that I rented out for ten years was a horrific reminder of the abuse that unfolded.

For ten years, I drove back to that house to visit my family members who rented it and every time, as I passed a farmer's yard, I would flash back to the night I escaped from him. When he had become so unhinged that I feared for my life.

Financial abuse is not something that I'd heard spoken about and so I just felt stupid. I felt to blame and guilty and that everyone would also think this of me. From being someone who always knew where and how I was spending my money, without even realising I had no access to *our* bank account. The staff at Barclays must have thought that I was insane. I was forever ringing up or going into the branch to complain that I hadn't had a statement, why had my PIN changed without my permission and why did the PIN machine that I had to use to access my bank account continually fail to work properly? I ordered new ones repeatedly that didn't arrive. This went on for months. My wonderful husband would always pop to the bank for me and take my card, as it was easier, and then it wouldn't go back in my purse. I'd ask him to get a bank balance, but he would 'forget'.

When my eyes were finally opened to his deception, he had been pilfering money little and often from the account through regular cash back. He always had an answer if I questioned it, *'we needed cat food' 'it was for your work's night out...'*. I believed him.

His lowest point has got to be stealing from our own wedding guests. On the day of our wedding, around twenty cards went missing from the *Safe Post Box* that the hotel provided. I realised that cards were missing when I didn't have one from my Grandad. He had saved up £40 cash and, in Grandad style, would have chosen a beautiful card with a beautiful message. My mum had put the card in the pillar box, so I knew it was gone. I made a *Monica-esque* spreadsheet to account for everyone's kind gifts and cards. Thankfully, several had put in cheques, but there was around £200 cash missing. The police were called, the hotel accused, and it was never solved. It had only ever been in the hotel safe during the reception and then given to the groom to store securely in our room.

It was several years after I escaped the relationship that it hit me... he had taken it. He had stolen from his own wedding, from his own family and from me. It still defies belief. This wasn't the only time that he stole from me, he stole my purse the night before I was going on a Hen do – with my Euros stashed inside. It disappeared off the dining room table (I know I left it there) and I can only assume that this was his way to try and stop me going.

But I didn't roll over and play victim. His attempts to socially isolate me weren't working. He tried to, and I can see that more now, but despite the emotional abuse, I still had my self-confidence and so I went anyway. You see, by then I had had my life-changing back operation and was off the opioids that had controlled my life for many years and so I was seeing much more clearly, had a lot of life to catch up with that I'd missed out on for eight years of chronic pain and I wasn't quite the victim that he had me pegged as.

I know now, looking back, that although my money story did play out pretty badly at times, it was my people pleasing ways and need for love and desperation for the perfect 2.4 family that was manipulated and allowed my trust to be destroyed. I was always doing what was best for the family, but in doing so, these two abusers had the perfect supply to feed their narcissistic tendencies and to take further advantage of me.

2020 brought me the breakdown that I needed in order to break free. Finally, after ten years I sold that picture-perfect dream home that became a living nightmare. Seeing that house go and finally freeing the ghosts that haunted its memory has left me feeling a lot lighter. I paid off the debt and started the next phase of my life, narcissist free. And more importantly, I began to rewrite my money story and reframe the limiting beliefs and guilt that had held me back for so long.

## Find your Money Story

I want you to think about your relationship with money. You may not have as obvious a story as mine, but I am sure that there will have been conversations and actions in your past that will have altered how you view money. Are we, as a society, open in talking about money? Do we tell each other our financial wins? From my teaching background, salary was never discussed, promotion increments were hush and people definitely did not celebrate being the top earners. Should this be different? Should we make it more acceptable to talk about and celebrate money? I know in the past two years so many people have lost businesses and it might feel wrong, but having a positive money mindset and discussing your financial rewards and wins is not the same as bragging, and if you think differently, maybe look at your own financial story and see if you can reframe that thinking.

I do know some people that have very strong, positive money mindsets, but more often in business, I come across people with similar stories to me, who struggle to charge their worth and the risk is that if you allow your money story to dictate your feelings towards money, you can become stuck in a scarcity mindset rather than a mindset of abundance.

Think about these questions in your family now and when you were a child.

Do you talk openly about money?

Is money a positive or negative thing in your life?

Were you brought up with any of these beliefs?

*Money doesn't grow on trees.*

*You have to work hard to make money.*

*Don't spend what you don't have.*

*Be happy with what you've got.*

*Time is money.*

*Money is the root of all evil.*

What are your first memories of money?

What was the state of your family's finances growing up?

Were you Wealthy/Comfortable/Poor?

How hard did your parents work to earn their money?

What thoughts did you have about rich people?

As an adult, what is your relationship with money?

Are you a saver?

Have you been in debt?

Do you spend easily/recklessly?

## Money Limiting Beliefs

Now, after answering these questions, I want you to think about your limiting beliefs surrounding money. These should come quickly and easy to you – don't overthink it.

Here are mine from when I did this task. *Money is evil, being rich is scary* and *I will never be rich*

Now, linking back to how we reframed limiting beliefs in the 'Self' chapter, we need to reframe these money beliefs. By reframing this negative thinking, *Money is evil* becomes *Money is safe*.

*Being rich is scary* becomes *Money brings opportunities* and *I will never be rich* becomes *I work hard and I am open to abundance*. Now that sounds better doesn't it!

Spend some time journaling on these points and re-write your story. You will be surprised what jumps out and I would love to hear them.

## Money Goals

If you are already in your own business, have a think about these questions.

*'How much do you want to earn in your first year?'* The first time I was asked this, I didn't have a clue. Yes of course I wanted to make money but actually saying it out loud was terrifying. This used to make me feel sick. I have had to work hard on my money mindset and I have made giant strides. Do you know what you want to earn?

*'How much are you going to charge for your course, membership, product?'* Money mindset has a lot to answer for when it comes to pricing the value of your product and setting yourself targets to work towards. Make sure you are pricing for your ideal client, not based on your money story and remember, whatever product or service you are selling... you are the expert so you aren't just charging for the hour, but for your knowledge, value and expertise!

I am setting you a challenge. From where you are now, whether that be already in business or ready to get started, put down on paper a goal of what you want to earn. Go for it! When a dream is written down it becomes a goal. Get it on your vision board, open yourself up to believing that you can do it and then set to work to make it happen! Part 2, *Increase your Impact,* will help you with that!

## Chapter 5
# Kindness

*"Healing doesn't mean the damage never existed. It means the damage no longer controls our lives."*

Being kind to yourself is one of the most important things and I don't just mean self-talk. We, as women, are masters of spinning all the plates and often, it is our plate that drops first - I know mine was.

When my depression and anxiety was at its worst, I can remember being in the outdoor spa jacuzzi and wanting it to swallow me up. I'd joined David Lloyd a few months earlier as a way to prioritise some time for me. Taking time for myself to exercise, to relax and to be alone whilst Emilie was in a class gave me some mental headspace, but it wasn't enough. I had been trying to rest and add self-care into my life but it was like I was swimming against the tide. It helped to an extent, and it probably held burnout at bay for a few more months at least, but by then, the emotional and mental exhaustion was too far gone.

Reclining back on the built-in spa bed, feeling the rejuvenating bubbles, smelling the crisp December air and gazing into a twilight sky – should have been bliss, but the darkness was palpable. Every bit of sunshine had faded from my life, and I can still remember the feeling of my face. Do you even feel your face? Usually, in day-to-day life, you don't walk around thinking, '*I have a face*' but when I was submerged in deep depression, I felt it all in my cheeks, my jowls, my chin. Some people call it the black dog, the cloud, for me it is like a balaclava of darkness.

Depression is the natural Botox as all ability to smile is lost. But unlike Botox, you can force a fake smile – but even with the fake smile, that feeling of deep sadness, blackness, trauma lived in every crease of my face, tone of voice and speed of talk. I don't know if anyone noticed my heavy expression, my sadness but I can certainly see the difference when I look back at photos. My eyes couldn't smile. Now they smile all the time. Yes, we can smile through the pain and sometimes we do have to put on a smile, but what we really want is to really smile. Smiling is scientifically good for you - it contributes to reducing your blood pressure, lowering stress hormones and boosting your mind.

In that jacuzzi, I only felt relaxed when I fully immersed my senses by putting my head under the water and filled my ears with water. The inner chatter of my mind was so loud, so constant, so deafening and draining. Lying back with my head in that water, with the jets booming underneath, the world was blocked out. I have no idea how long I lay there for. Sometimes fully submerged, other times just my ears, but I found a blackness. A quiet, safe blackness. Having been terrorised for nine months with flashbacks and nightmares, to be living the same trauma in sleep as awake; it was a relief to find nothing. That deep blackness, then never-ending vortex of safety pulled me under. I wanted to stay. I begged for the water to envelop me, to protect me from my senses and for once to keep my mind at bay. I had reached emotional and psychological burnt out. The over-giving, faking and constant triggers led me to that very dark place.

That's the closest I would say that I came to having suicidal thoughts. I would fantasise about being back in that blackness, where everything would stop. Where the pain would end. Where I didn't need to be the survivor. Was I suicidal? I didn't think so – but that disclosure in my emergency occupational health appointment meant that finally I told someone how I truly felt. She was the first one to help me out of that dark pool because despite everything that I know about mental health, when I was in it, I couldn't ask for help. I was screaming inside for people to notice but I was putting on such a good show of *'super mum, super teacher'* that when I stopped and allowed myself to ask for help, I broke. And then I broke some more.

## Burnout isn't a badge of honour

Burnout was not something that I really knew about. I knew I was knackered a lot of the time - I was a teacher and a solo mum after all - and over the years had felt burnt out, but *Burnout* was a whole other level! Burnout is a state of emotional, physical and mental exhaustion caused by excessive and prolonged stress. It occurs when you feel overwhelmed, emotionally drained and unable to meet constant demands. The impact on life can be extreme, from the primary damage being emotional, leading to anxiety disorder, detachment and depression, it contributes to making life not seem like living and includes a loss of motivation, ideals, hope and an increase in illness, irritability, isolation withdrawal. I had all of these.

For the last few years, I have referred to that time as my *'breakdown'* but when I heard Roxy Rhodes speak whilst on a recent *Ladies Life Lounge* retreat, she said something that stuck with me. She spoke about the fact that our system doesn't break. We are not broken. Our central nervous and emotional system has simply got to a point where it needs to rest because we have reached a very dark, low place that probably feels the lowest it ever has. She was right. I didn't break, but I did have burnout and a recent therapist explained that the state that I described being in as emotional and psychological burnout, yet the GP signed me off with anxiety. Where was the understanding? This was so much more that feeling anxious but at that time, I didn't have any fight or positivity in me. What I needed was to rest.

I know now that if we don't make the choice to stop and rest, eventually our body and mind will make that decision for us. But when we are living in survival mode, it can feel impossible to stop, and rest can be illusive. Often, when we need it the most, sleep evades us. When your mind is whirling with anxiety and worry, even sleep isn't restful and add to that the stresses of jobs, children, divorce, court, house moves, and pandemics, then burnout is certainly calling.

We know that babies, toddler and children don't sleep as well if they are over-tired, yet we perpetually stretch ourselves to the limit. And let's not forget those of us battling sleep deprivation due to children. I stood in solidarity with you for over two years, the original glazed walking dead look, and aroma of coffee was my day-to-day roll. Emilie had reflux and sleep was pretty much non-existent for a long time. It is no surprise that sleep deprivation is a form of torture as it takes away so much from you. But as much as we know sleep deprivation is awful, it does seem to become some sort of badge of honour that we use to *prove* that we are doing everything, giving everything and being everything for our children. I know I was guilty of this. Yes, it's fine to vent on social media and compare notes on whose life is worst. Asking for help is not a sign of weakness, especially if carrying on without is to the detriment of your own wellbeing. If you need to rest, you need to rest. Non-negotiable.

Sleep boosts your immune system. Major restorative function in the body such as tissue repair, muscle growth, and protein synthesis occur almost exclusively during sleep. If you are in a relaxed state of mind, your brain is most likely to give you your best, most creative ideas. Rest helps us to have a calmer and clearer mind, encouraging positive thinking, concentration, memory and decision making. When we rest, our bodies repair themselves from daily wear and tear.

Rest allows time for reflection and allows us to evaluate our goals and priorities. When we relax, the flow of blood increases around our body, giving us more energy and your "feel-good" hormones a chance to be released. I did rest. I slept. I didn't get dressed, I lay on the sofa, but I still tried not to feel. Gradually, over the months, I started to see glimmers of myself and that was when I started to listen to *The Secret*.

The mum juggle will continue and so the onus is now, more than ever, on us as women, to set our non-negotiables, to set boundaries and to prioritise our own self-care.

## Time to Ignite

As my Relax Kids business grew, I began to realise that it was mums that were crying out support as well as their children. When I started my first Facebook group, I began to share the mindfulness techniques that had helped me. At this point I met Niki Kinsella. From her, I learned all about the Chakras of the body and became interested in the chakras and the elements. We are surrounded by key elements in life, five elements of the body namely - Earth, Water, Fire, Air and Space.

In order to ignite, we need to connect with all five elements, in order to align, body and mind. These elements maintain balance, and if any one of these elements are taken out, the body would collapse. Imbalances of these five elements can trigger illness and disease and so I began to create my own signature system so that, through *Mamas Ignited,* I could support women who were struggling with depression, burnout and setting their non-negotiables. These elements became linked to the techniques of grounding, massage, stretch, breathing and visualisation. This was also something that I was using daily with Emilie. This led to me creating and delivering my first signature course and book of the same name.

## The Juggle-struggle

By creating, using and embodying the *Ignite system,* I managed the juggle struggle of the pandemic and emerged like a butterfly - calm and serene and ready to rediscover the beauty of the world. I believe that if I hadn't made these proactive changes, my story now would be much different.

This is something that we all have to be reminded - Be kind to yourself. Make time for self-care and make it your non-negotiable. Your life, family and business will only thrive if you take time to look after you. Don't get sucked under by the juggle-struggle. Take that walk, sit for lunch, go to the gym or if all else fails, lock the door to the bathroom – whatever it is be kind to you.

When I was writing an article for *The Capsule,* I found startling statistics about the intense knock-on effect of Covid-19 on the childcare and household roles between men and women. Lockdown held up a mirror to family set ups and highlighted a huge imbalance nationwide.

A Mumsnet survey of more than 1,500 women found that 79% agreed that *"responsibility for home schooling fell largely to me"* and 77% agreed that *"It was impossible for me to work uninterrupted"* when schools closed.

The juggle-struggle over the last two years has been more obvious than ever - women are doing it all. The statistics clearly show that women were more likely to be having to accommodate time for home-schooling in the day, meaning that many were working late into the evening. So, what did we learn from the pandemic? The truth weighs heavily in my mind - roles are still not equal for many men and women. So, what to do about all this?

The way I see it is that the new gender equality is about deciding on roles within the home that are formed by communication and compromise, rather than expectation. So, if equality is being compromised then who is to blame? We need to be able to confidently have conversations to allow us to share the load of the childcare, housework and daily drudgery, otherwise are we perpetuating the age-old stereotypes? Not always as easy as it sounds. Generations of expectation and acceptance may need to be challenged with difficult conversations, but in the here and now, if those conversations don't happen, there won't be balance.

## Set your non-negotiable

Is there a non-negotiable in your week? Is there something that you do for you? It has to be something without the kids, time for you and it has to be a regular fixture in your life. It could be exercise, nails, a coffee – but you must make it non-negotiable. If not, make it happen.

Of course, I am writing this as a solo mum who struggles to keep everything spinning, but my non-negotiable is my cleaner!

If you can take only one piece of advice away from this book it is this... Ditch the guilt and get a cleaner (if you haven't already seen the light). Joanne is a part of my team and without her, the house literally goes to shit! Even working from home, I struggle to keep on top of everything and delegating that part of the running of the household and making an exchange of money is magical.

As the house stays clean, it takes away my anxiety that I'm not good enough. I struggle to look after the house. I've felt guilty for years -especially when I was on maternity leave. As skint as I was, I wish I'd swapped a takeaway for a cleaner – I would have been a lot happier. You're not lazy, you are making an active decision for *you* and ultimately, your mental health.

Taking time for *you* can be the maker rather than the breaker. Instilling a simple mindfulness routine to your day can give you the space and time to be. How can you stop and just be in the moment? Try having a bath with candles and relaxing music. Download a mindfulness or meditation app and switch off. Discover Reiki – you won't regret it. Try Yoga or Pilates – it hurts but your mind will thank you.

Just please, be kind to yourself. Look out for the signs of burnout and depression and reach out for help. Taking time to rest, to just be and to heal, can be hard but like anything, it needs practice. Slowly, the symptoms will lesson, your days will become brighter and eventually you won't be able to remember the last time you cried.

## Find the Silence

As you already know, woo was not my thing and so when I reached burnout, as a full-time teacher with a four your old in tow, there was very little silence. I used to stay up super late just because it was the only silence that I got, but this was counter-productive as I was so burnt out and needed the sleep. If I am honest, this still happens now as that silence is just everything. The difference to now though, is that I work from home, so I don't crave the silence like I used to. Plus, I have implemented ways into my life to allow my mind some quiet. This is still a work in progress and that healing journey doesn't end, but learning how to breathe, to stretch, to visualise and to *just be* was a game-gamer.

Have a think about the time that you take each day that is just for you to connect body and mind and just be. This may be something that you work into your non-negotiable moving forward. Whether this be a meditation, five minutes brew in peace or a hot bath – silence and allowing yourself space from the juggle-struggle of life is needed. Quite often, mine is ten minutes sitting in the car when I get home from the school run. I know that once I get into the house there is an endless list of *stuff* to be done, so those minutes of stillness in the car work for me.

Visualisation is powerful technique that I use with clients and the children that I have worked with. Creating an image in your head and allowing yourself to visualise that place, space, feeling or emotion not only calms your nervous system but can reprogramme negative thoughts. Think back to the vision boards. By visualising your future, you can begin to believe and create intention to make it happen. Creating a relaxing, positive or safe mental image to induce a feeling is just as effective.

By imagining something, you are able to trick the brain, as research shows that the brain does not know the difference between real and imagined scenarios. We can visualise a place, a feeling, a result. This is very powerful. Think about athletes – Mo Farah is open about his use of visualisation and how he visualises winning and the positive outcome. This can be transferred to your life. Visualise yourself in a safe, happy place or a place of confidence and victory.

There are also lots of guided visualisations that you can listen to that take you through an imagined place or journey and these are wonderful to do before sleep. Ask Alexa to play *'Unicorn Magic'* - we both love it.

Meditation is a state of deep peace. Meditations can be used by repeating words or mantras, staring at a specific object, breathing deeply or focussing on one individual thought. I am not an expert and there are many people that I can point you towards, such as the aforementioned Niki Kinsella and Claire Morton, aka *The Purpose Pusher*. I love Claire's approach as she gives you an honest approach to making meditation work for you and how it can easily be slotted into your day. She starts by asking you to close your eyes and be aware of what you can see, then hear, smell, taste and touch. Initially, you think about them each in turn and then, as you move deeper into relaxation, you can focus on them all interchangeably at the same time. Just one minute of meditation has proven health benefits. I encourage you to give it a try and find the way that works for you.

Meditation for me still feels scary and unsafe, because this is when the feelings come. When I allow myself to sit in my own space and feel my own feelings, it is tough. Thoughts that arose once during a meditation triggered me and took me back to that dark place again, but I know that if I keep stamping on these feelings, one day they will erupt. My self-awareness and self-compassion have improved so much since I began my therapy and coaching journey after the assault, and I want you to know that if it does seem impossible, if you feel like you will never change and you will never feel happy, safe and empowered… you will… but like anything, your mental health needs working on and to be match fit, we have to put the training in.

## How do you *Just Be* if you don't know how?

If you have been though any sort of trauma or adversity, you will know that you are in a constant state of doing. You keep doing, aka fighting, so that you don't have to stop and deal with the thing. But what you really need to do is *feel the feels* and stop doing, so that you can deal with the thing. I'm sorry to say that I do not have all of the answers and after a recent therapy session, I know that I still have months of intensive therapy ahead of me. I nearly stopped writing this book as a giant dollop of imposter syndrome landed and my limiting beliefs told me that '*I was a complete fraud'* and *'I had no right to even try and help people when I am such a massive fuck up'*. Of course, I reframed these and finished the book but I know that I still have to work on slowing down and being silent to process my ongoing thoughts and feelings.

On the outside, I am MAMAS IGNITED - in giant yellow letters. I am the fire and the spark and the passion. I am the face of the brand and show up - doing, doing, doing. Doing is what I am best at. Being... not so much.

Lockdown one proved that. When I was left alone with just my own thoughts and company for six months, I was left naked and wide open to having to deal with my pain and trauma. So, what did I do? Started crafting like a mad woman, became home schoolteacher of the year... uploading ALL the work onto the school system so that I (I mean Emilie, of course) would get the praise and validation for the work. She (I) even achieved Star of the WEEK – my god, that got me through a few more days.

I can look back now and see that I couldn't just *be*. I thought I was. I thought I had a handle on things but what I was doing was self-soothing with lots of alcohol and food. Now, I could use the sweeping statement that *'It was Lockdown'* and yes, I know many, many people that were doing the same. But for me, it wasn't about the boredom of lockdown, or the extended party atmosphere, it was about closing the void that lockdown had brought as I was no longer do, do, doing.

Thankfully, the Relax Kids training came along and I began to learn all about mindfulness and found the techniques that I needed to start to heal myself.

## Thought dump

Journaling is a great way to offload thoughts and emotions. It can be used in a way to suit you and doesn't have to by diary style. Journals with prompts are available and can help to focus your thinking. If you are feeling overwhelmed or upset, writing is a good way to unpick these emotions.

As a child, I often wrote a diary but was never consistent. I went for years, religiously writing one and then would lose the flow. They were more 'what I did today' diaries and I was never free to fully divulge my free feelings and emotions because I was always terrified that my sister would find it or, even worse, my mum and dad!

I never journaled until I saw a counsellor for the first time, during my marriage. I began seeing her when I was trying to make sense of what was going on in my marriage. I was so heavily gaslighted that I had almost lost sense of what was real. I had been longing for this happy ending for so long and when it was there, gifted to me, I would have done anything to keep it. So, somehow, I was able to mask the red flags, to hear the lies and swallow it as truth, to admit that I was the one going crazy rather than face up to the harsh truth of what was going on.

Sit back and watch you own life. Stop doing, start observing. This was what helped me to lift my head enough to spot one lie, and then another, and so it went on.

It was my journal that also helped me to unravel the tangled web of my own thoughts and feelings. The two became so interwoven that it was hard to know what my actual feelings were.

## Kindness

One day, I broke down in tears at school. I ended up in the school Chapel, crying and completely unable to express why I was crying. I didn't know. I just knew that there was a pain and a grief that I needed to let go.

When I was planning my escape, I went to Manchester and stayed in a hotel for a week as I was marking for the exam board and the hotel was a bonus. The clarity that I found there with my journal allowed me to plan my escape in a safe and strategic way. Setting up a new bank account and finding somewhere to live being the priorities. Yet when I went back home and he was there, just being in his presence brought a fog into my head. He was so intense, and I became claustrophobic. I lived with him for two weeks under the pretence that we were trying to fix things. I asked him to sleep in the spare room to give me space, but I would wake up to find him sitting watching me sleep. Items around the house would be smashed in the night. I can remember the intense fear hearing him smashing things, to which he denied all knowledge. I was the mad one.

Writing in my journal allowed me to be able to preserve the truth and remember my true thoughts and feelings so that when he did begin to suffocate me, I had that beacon of hope and reminder that I was going to escape.

And an escape it was. When I eventually told him that it was over, he had already twigged and was already spiralling out of control. He knew when my wages didn't go into our joint account that I was onto him. He had been slowly pilfering money from the account for so long that I had got used to being perpetually skint. He always had an answer for where the money had gone... the cats was usually his excuse!

Telling him that it was over on my own was a huge mistake. After the intense future faking declarations and promises, he very soon became deranged - At one point, pinning me down on the sofa, to chasing me with a knife where I had to hide in the bathroom and ring the police.

He was reported to the police, I made a statement, and they were ready to send me home with no charges. The older police offer said, *'if you need us again just ring 999, keep your phone close.'* Thankfully, the younger of two was not happy with this and offered to escort me home to retrieve my belongings. In his words, *'if he comes at you again with a knife, 999 can't save you. It's only a house. Your life is way more important.'*

That Police officer potentially saved my life because when we returned to the house, by that point, he was very drunk and for the first time, I saw the true monster that he was. He looked different, his mannerisms were different, he even stood differently. It was like he had taken the costume of my husband off to reveal the true dangerous monster underneath.

A few weeks later, he plotted to trap me in the house. He used his mum as a decoy and succeeded in trapping me in the bedroom with him. When faced with what I knew to be my abuser rather than my husband, he looked, smelled, and spoke differently. His whole demeanour was that of someone else. I had been living with a stranger.

If this was a storyline on a soap opera, it would seem far-fetched. But this was my life. Somehow, I evaded him and fled from the house with him pursuing me. Slamming doors and knocking things over, in true movie style, I had to get to my car which was parked across the street. As a pulled the door shut, his arm reached in and grabbed the steering wheel. I beeped the horn incessantly and screamed so loud and began somehow to drive. His arm slipped away, and I was free. The terror that I felt in that moment, with my husband in our dream home, was, at that point, the most terrified I had ever been. I have never seen him since.

I left and never looked back.

This isn't all accounted in my journal. I didn't diarise that day - I didn't need to. As with all trauma, it is etched into your being. I have re-read my journals recently and I see a damaged, desperate women with no clue how to deal with what happened. That girl, who had been searching for the *Happy Ever After,* had been left destroyed. But sadly, back then nobody - including myself - spoke about this being domestic abuse. The term 'psycho' was bandied around but what had happened was I had been emotionally, psychologically and financially abused by him. It took eight years and another abusive relationship before I realised.

## Your journal

I could regale you with stories of my past for another ten pages, but what I want is for you to think about how you can help yourself to *Just be.* Journaling is an excellent tool to help you and if you struggle to know where to start, here are some prompts for you:

What my life is now…

What my life could be…

My hopes are…

This brings us to the end of SPARK. When I say *Ignite your Spark*, I want it to be tangible advice that you can take forward with you. I want you to be able take action. Do you feel excited? Allowing yourself to want more is exciting, liberating and terrifying all at the same time, but it can be done.

Come and join me in Part Two – FIRE, and I will help you to take those important steps into making that spark ignite. I have clients that are at the very start of their journey and women that are more established in business. Whatever stage you are at, we will create the foundations… and then it is time for action. So, pack that ironing board away. Let's surf.

## Part Two
# Surf The Fire

*"If you really want to do something, you'll find a way. If you don't, you'll find an excuse."*

— Jim Rohn

Ok, so we have been through *Ignite your Spark* and I have unloaded a lot of my shit onto you. I have no doubt made you think about lots of your own shit and I am sorry if anything has triggered you, but I hope that you have set aside some time, to journal, to just be, have set your non-negotiables and above all, know that you want more from life. It could be a change of gear in many different ways - and don't forget that vision board. Get clear on your goals for this next year. Be intentional and keep living in that positive mindset.

What I want you to know is that the Louisa in these stories doesn't exist anymore. She is a new, much shinier version. A favourite line that my first boyfriend used to say is *'You can't polish a turd... but you can roll it in glitter.'* This always made me laugh, and without getting too carried away with a poo analogy, for a long time, I was that poo rolled in glitter. I looked sparkly and happy on the outside but inside felt like... you guessed it, shit. December 2018, I was playing a comedic role in White Christmas – a musical that personifies Christmas and all things happy. Every night on stage I smiled, danced, made the audience laugh and cracked jokes galore backstage. Then I would go home and cry. Gripped with despair, anxiety and fear in the life that I was living, the escape of the theatre being my solitude. The problem with being a good actress is when you become an actress in real life too and, for far too long, I acted okay. As Robin Williams famously said;

*"Nobody fakes being depressed. They fake being okay."*

Not anymore.

There is only so long that you can cover up the cracks and you have to do the inner work. When I started to focus on what was underneath the glitter, that was when the good stuff started. This is still a work in progress, but this book isn't about being the polished turd, it is about making the changes from the inside out and knowing that you will always have to work on something but it is getting started that is the most important.

This section will refer more specifically to anyone running or wanting to launch a business, but please remember that all of the messages and inner work applies to making a change in all parts of your life. You could be applying for a dream job, wanting to break free from a toxic friendship and this could be the very start of you realising that there is something in your life that doesn't serve you and making the decision to go for it. To go for it, you need to take action, and then you will rise and make your own ripples.

So here we are. You have done the work, you have admitted that you want more, so let's get you out there. If you are starting a business, launching something new or wanting to raise your profile, the only way to do that is to get in view, to get seen and get heard. If you have been hiding away, like many of us do when in states of freeze, then this can be tough. But you have something special to share, you have a spark that will no longer be dampened.

This section is more than just jumping on your surfboard. It is about jumping on your surfboard despite the fear, trauma, expectation or limiting beliefs that have kept you small. It is the choice to no longer be shackled to your past, to no longer recreate generational cycles of abuse, trauma and people pleasing tendencies. To say *no* to your inner critic and release your guilt, pain and yes, you guessed it again... fear.

## Chapter 6
# Fear

*"Don't be ashamed of your story. It will inspire others."*

If you are going to a job interview then the first thing that you will do is think about your outfit, your appearance. First impressions and all that! (Don't worry I won't lecture you on time keeping... once I was forty-five minutes late for an interview and amazingly still got the job!)

So many women in business that I work with are afraid to put themselves in full view on their personal Facebook profiles. I get it. We have already spoken about fears and judgement... but now is the time to put away those fears and trust that the right people will be watching and that if you speak to the people that you want to serve then the people that it doesn't apply to will work out it isn't for them.

Advertisers still advertise make-up even though it will only apply to one corner of the market. Your social media is the same.

Yes, your old mates from school might not want to listen to your lives about setting boundaries, but that mate from your old job just might.

So why do we fear getting in view? Yes, you guessed it, fear can often stem back to childhood and those limiting beliefs again.

Can you remember a time in your childhood where you wanted to shrivel away? Where you wanted to hide and the floor to just swallow you up? I can. It was backstage at the Theatre Royal in St. Helens, for my annual Ballet showcase. My group were doing the Sailor's Hornpipe, complete with full sailor outfit. As I'd always had short hair, I never had a bun like the other girls and had to scrape my hair in a hairnet. I was also much taller than the other girls in my class.

I could see a group of girls in the older group looking over and sniggering. One of the girls was pushed to come over. She came over and I instantly felt uncomfortable. She looked me up and down and said, *"We all want to know... are you a he or a she?"* and then they all laughed.

I was mortified, I wanted to disappear. I didn't tell anyone, I held onto the pain and swallowed it down.

This never held me back as a child, I'm glad to say. I was always more than happy to be in view, on the stage taking the limelight. Drama at University nurtured this love and my side-line of extra work is still my 'claim to fame'. Signed up with an agency, I was a regular on Brookside, Hollyoaks and Emmerdale, along with some serial dramas. The excitement of working on location and in the studio made my spark of desire to work in TV burn like an inferno.

My claim to fame is having two (small) speaking parts on Hollyoaks and a featured role on Emmerdale. Whilst completing the MA in TV scriptwriting, I applied for countless jobs at Mersey and Yorkshire TV... from story liner to minibus driver! I fantasised about writing for Emmerdale and moving to Leeds. I even managed an invite to the Brookside and Hollyoaks Christmas Party, as it was the night I'd been filming my part as a nurse... cue famous line, *"Will you keep the noise down please!"* (Adam's car crash when he was paralysed, for any avid Hollyoaks fans circa 2002). I chatted to directors and writers, and I just knew in my gut that this was my purpose.

I have always been confident when it comes to getting up on stage. I really do not care what people think. I was a member of a musical theatre company for years and played many parts and I thrived on it. But somehow, getting visible online is a whole other beast. Speaking and the fear of judgement was holding me back. Due to my mental health and my anxiety and paranoia, it was much easier to delete everyone and hide, which I did for a while. Hiding away is often much safer. But in hiding, it keeps you stuck where you are. When I decided to form *Mamas Ignited*, I found it difficult to get in view.

But how could I launch a business if nobody could see me?

My first live was on my first ever online challenge with Dani Wallace. I was sat slumped, wearing my grey hoodie, wanting to blend in with the grey sofa, but sharing a small part of my story and receiving so much support from other women changed everything. Yet again, I felt that spark come to life. Dani, aka *The Queen Bee,* has been instrumental in helping me to step into my power. She is my mentor and my friend and is a blazing example of someone who personifies her brand. She showed me that despite the adversity and limiting beliefs, I could #FLYANYWAY.

When I joined the challenge, I wasn't visible in the online space. I was aware of Dani, as I'd met her at Womanifest, but hadn't found the courage to make myself visible. I was hiding, fearful and terrified of judgment. I knew I wanted *more* and I had started, but I was self-sabotaging and keeping myself small.

I had been visible online regarding Relax Kids classes, but telling my own story was a whole other issue. I had joined Jane Louise Pattison and Lioness to write my story, but I didn't dare tell anyone. My very first vulnerable step was only a month before publication, when I told a few close people that I was in a book that was soon to be published. I was an English teacher and I was terrified to tell people that I was going to be a published author. How crazy is that?

On deadline day, I was stalling. I was so afraid to press send. I took a deep breath and wrote a post on Facebook… telling everyone that I had written a chapter in a book called '*Pride*' and was living my dream. If I hadn't written that post that day, I might not have sent the email. I could have stepped away from that amazing opportunity because of fear.

I can remember the panic and anxiety in my chest, struggling to breathe as I pressed send, but it was a powerful step that has carried me to where I am now and that ripple continues.

If nothing changes, nothing changes. I felt broken but taking control of my life and taking that step was the best thing I ever did. The support I got back was unbelievable.

The following week, I received an email from Dani, telling me that her challenge was opening soon. I signed up, I showed up and the rest is history.

## When does Fear kick in?

How does fear show up in your life? Is there something new and exciting that you'd love to try but you don't because of fear? Is there something that you have never tried because of fear or, even worse, the fear of judgement? This is what I was afraid of. I was afraid as I knew that some people at work would judge me. I am not sure what they judged me on, but the complete lack of discussion of the book showed that I was right. My fear of judgement lasted for a long time.

As kids we are totally fearless. We can climb, fall, run, jump all without fear. We trust, we don't judge, and we are innocent. When does it change? When does the fear kick in? I can certainly remember feeling nervous when I was performing and there was an element of fear, but I did it anyway!

When I was five, I won a singing competition at *Rockley Sands Holiday Park* in Poole. I can remember the nerves as I sang, *Do-re-mi* and the fear as the piano didn't sound the same as it did in the film... and a little lost without Julie Andrews to carry my tiny voice.

I was all alone, on stage, with hundreds of eyes on me. I was terrified. I can remember the feel of my silk dress and the encouraging nod from the pianist who, no doubt, was following me rather than the other way round. From a nervous start, I did it and I was filled with confidence. When I finished, the crowd erupted and soon after, I was presented with the trophy and the prize of a free holiday to return for the grand final.

I have no memory at all of the final. Needless to say, I went and I sang but I have no personal recollection of the night. I didn't win, but I do remember snippets of the holiday. It just goes to show that the positive memory far outweighs the negative!

Sometimes in life, we are afraid to do things that put us out of our comfort zone. We are afraid to get in view in case we make a fool of ourselves. Ironically, now I don't have any confidence in my singing voice but over the years, I sang anywhere and everywhere. As a child I had no fear, and I always knew that I wanted to be more.

I wanted to be a singer (like Kylie) or a model or a TV presenter. I believed that I could do ANYTHING, but over time, we start to lose that non-wavering self-belief. Knocks along the way affect our self-esteem and we can often find ourselves tucked away in a place of safety that doesn't serve us or make us happy.

After Dani's challenge, I decided to stop letting the fear hold me back. I held my breath and jumped onto her Speaker Mastermind, *Bee Inspired*. Six months to learn all about public speaking, to craft and then deliver a talk, tapping into my story to inspire an audience. Yep, I ditched the fear and jumped in headfirst. I felt like that five-year-old girl again. I was scared but excited and I knew that I could do it, even if I didn't have Julie Andrews up there with me. That spark had already ignited in me and I was ready to rise and surf through the fire... but the only problem was, I didn't know how to surf.

This is where my chosen mentors, Dani and Jo Swann, guided, pushed and lifted me up until I could see that I always knew how to surf, I just need that encouragement. My personal development journey and working with amazing mentors has helped me to overcome limiting beliefs, to understand my authentic self (still working on that) and to not be afraid to be unapologetically me. People might still judge me, but that is none of my business anymore.

We can actively train ourselves to *feel the fear and do it anyway*. Affirmations, power music and dancing are what help to alleviate my nerves. When I was on *Bee Inspired*, I was challenged by Dani to choose a Power song and I chose '*Waka Waka*' by Shakira. It reminds me of a crazy night, singing karaoke in a bar in Hong Kong and just always lifts me up. It is now mine and Emilie's power song and if ever I feel the nerves before a live, a launch or a challenge, I play it SOO loud, open up my arms above my head in my favourite power pose and breathe away the fear. Visualise the fear leaving your body as you exhale, shake your booty and smile. Trust me, it works.

Power Poses were something new that I discovered. Amy Cuddy does a great TedX on this. Hold your chest open, hands on hips, or up in a V shape in the air and you feel like you can conquer the world. Body language has a lot to say about how you are feeling and can instantly lift your mood.

## Women having power over themselves

When I was at university, studying BA English Literature, there was a very obvious thread throughout my choices of modules, essays and dissertation. Feminism. Feminism wasn't something that I was fully aware of, apart from my A Level teacher and our wonderful study of 'The Handmaid's Tale', which remains my favourite book of all time (if you are ever in a Mr and Mrs quiz with me). Miss Midmer's zest and passion for literature, right back to Tess of the D'Ubervilles at GCSE, is what lit my spark and love for literature. In a beautiful serendipity moment, Allyson (then Midgely) was my PGCE tutor and a very fitting way to enter my teaching career, as it was down to her that my spark became a blaze. Don't get me wrong, I had always been a reader and a writer, but her passion just astounded me. I can remember listening to her with such amazement and wonder when she would analyse text, wondering how on earth she could know that. Fast forward twenty years and I have stood in that same spot, and I know I have inspired students in the same way that she inspired me. Many, many pupils over the years have gone on to study Literature, or have even just passed English, and have accredited it to me. That is the one true joy of teaching and one that I miss.

There I was at university, without the apron strings of Miss Midmer and a world of theory. I devoured the feminist theory and began to form my own opinions and beliefs about the world and how women have been treated. In my essays and debates, I was always so forthright with my opinions, yet this never transcended into my life. I was never one to rock or the boat or speak out on politics, sexism, racism until the last few years. I expect the people-pleasing part in me wanted to remain safe and so any strong beliefs were kept as my own inner beliefs.

That is until I stepped in Dani Wallace's world. From the ashes I felt this rebirth of the Louisa from university – the one who knew the things but was afraid to say the things. *'Life was Simpler when Women Knew their Place'* was the title of my talk and there I was, with my ironing board and 1950s housewife attire, sharing some harsh truths about post-pandemic mental health, the juggle-struggle faced by women and the modern need for balance and difficult conversations.

In the words of Emma Watson, 'If you stand for equality, then you're a feminist. Sorry to tell you.' Don't be afraid to stand up and speak about what you believe in.

Just a year before, I was terrified at the thought of people judging me. By April 2021 I was surfing my ironing board in the centre of Warrington, on lives and on the *Bee Inspired* stage. But I wasn't just surfing it literally, that surfboard metaphor goes much deeper. By standing up for what I truly believed, writing and publishing, I was finally following the dream. As soon as I began to realise that by showing up as my authentic self, the more I realised that I had something to special to share.

I was finally living my purpose!

I was no longer living in fear. I was ignited.

## Chapter 7
# Ignite

*"Do not judge me by successes, judge me by how many times I fell down and got back up again."*

— Nelson Mandela

I always wanted more from life. I was never happy to just settle for the normal and from a young age, I had a fire inside me. From modelling at the age of two, to winning the singing competition aged five, I was *'destined for bigger things'*. If you asked me what I wanted to do when I was older, it was more I knew what I didn't want to do. I knew I wouldn't be in a *'boring 9-5'*. I had ambition to be more. Writing was my first love and my Saturday afternoons were spent in WH Smith, browsing the books (treating it like a library) and fantasising about moving to America and being a published author with my best friend and fellow English teacher, Sarah.

Around age fourteen, I decided that I wanted to be a children's TV presenter and I found out that I'd need to be a journalist, so this was my career. I was going to be a journalist, to write for a living and make it in TV. That was the plan. I could never see myself married with kids. My visions of the future were about being famous, travelling, being a writer and living an exciting life.

After university, as my friends who had been my world for three years all returned to their various parts of the country, I found myself with the biggest hangover. Leaving university and the infinite possibilities of the future left me feeling bereft. I had a 2:1 degree in English and Drama but I felt like a jack of all trades; master of none. This was when I joined a Master of Arts Degree in *Television and Radio Scriptwriting* and it was like I came home. The course was part-time over two years, so delivered one Thursday evening a week. For the rest of the time, I was working in a call centre where I ended up with an accidental career in travel, where I was promoted and found myself in a sales team leader job. It was like I was Clark Kent, leading a double life. By day I was on the phones, coaching my teams, running recruitment centres and delivering buzz sessions and by night I was a superhero... a budding writer saving the world with the power of my pen.

My spark was so bright that I didn't even doubt that I had the ability. I worked in London on countless unpaid *Runner* jobs for the experience and slept on floors galore. I was being pulled more and more towards the path that I wanted, yet the pull from home and my then boyfriend was so hard. Writing lit me up and when that spark went out, I wondered for a very long time if it could ever reignite. I realise now that it didn't extinguish fully, but years of pain, trauma, limiting beliefs and adversity meant that it was easier and safer to put up my ironing board and play safe.

## Setting up the Ironing Board

For many years it felt that when I became a teacher, I forfeited my passion. Why did I stop writing? I wanted to write. I used to enter short film competitions, I was shortlisted and had one-to-one sessions at Granada, I had scripts recommended to the BBC by my tutors. I was good. But I lost it. I lost my nerve, lost my passion and stopped doing. The trauma of my parents' breakup, breaking off my engagement and subsequent run away meant that I lost my purpose and it is only now that the spark is fully ignited and this time, it is blazing.

Looking back, it now seems that all good intentions of writing were packed up in the PGCE enrolment pack. On my first day on the PGCE, the words of a cynical ex rattled around my head, *'Those who can, do; those who can't, teach.'* But after twelve months of running and having a whole lot of fun, it was time to grow up. Too many nights out, too many hangovers, no money and no prospects. What did I love doing? Reading and writing. So why not combine this love and teach. *And with all those holidays*, I could easily carry on writing in the holidays. I could take my laptop abroad and write a bestseller whilst sipping Sex on the Beach – this was the lie that I told myself as the course unfolded in front of me.

As I climbed the teaching ladder to Head of Year and Head of Faculty, along with planning and delivering Outstanding lessons and OFSTED observations, my creative mind was lost. Lost under piles of marking, schemes, of work and excuses. Excuses. Why was I not been writing? Fear? Laziness? Life? Striving for the next promotion, searching for the perfect relationship, and planning the next big holiday, have all got in the way. Did I waste the last sixteen years? Does being a teacher make you a failure in your own field? Surely not?

Teaching brought with it so many challenges, successes and ultimately, job satisfaction that I could never have imagined. The joy of helping a child to succeed and fulfil their potential. To be told your lesson makes English fun, to meet parents and know that you have made a difference to their children's lives, to have a job that counts. How can this be '*not doing?*' I may not have been a famous writer, have fulfilled my dream of journalism or become a TV presenter, but apart from the ever-expanding paper trail and the ever-increasing demands for results, I found a job and a career that I loved. A passion not just for English, but for children and for nurturing those children. It is the students that count, and I know that my teaching has inspired and developed young people's minds. Ironically, I was never looking for a '*get out*'.

Over the years, no matter how many promotions I was given, there was always a niggle. I loved teaching but was this my true purpose? I had never wanted to be a teacher. I know I took the safe, sensible option but it was never a calling. I was a bloody good teacher because I loved my subject and I cared about the pupils. I cared about the whole child, their mental well-being as well as their academic ability and so, in a round-about way teaching has brought me full circle back to that *sliding door*... and when I finally found the power in me to open the door, it was waiting for me.

In the two years before having Emilie, I was Head of English and part of the leadership team opening and recruiting for a new

University Technical College. It was the best and worst of times and I shed blood, sweat and many tears during my time there. I had a bloody awful pregnancy and didn't have that 'pregnancy glow'. By the time she arrived, I was already shattered after nine months of teaching, morning sickness, gestational diabetes and the thing that finally finished me off... pelvic girdle pain. As my surgeon said, 'With the make up of your spine it was inevitable.' I was signed off at twenty-four weeks and started what felt like the Green Mile to Motherhood. She was so wanted and so loved, but I had no clue how to carry on my life with a baby in tow. My purpose had totally changed.

When Emilie was born and I became a Mummy, I finally achieved the 2.4 dream but in doing so, I lost myself for a while. My purpose completely changed. For ten years I had been a teacher and a leader for other people. My life had revolved around my job and my weekend social life. Years of nights out, hangovers, work, marking and planning. I could work when I wanted, say yes to any invitation, nip off on holiday at the drop of a hat - and believe me, I did. It only took the sniff of a holiday for me to be off and away. Suddenly I was in a new leadership role, but one that I was not prepared for.

## The Smiling Darkness of Motherhood

We hear all about the rush of oxytocin; the life changing moment and I felt it all. I was deliriously happy but in no way prepared for what was to come. I didn't know how to just be a Mum. How to cope with a new-born and where to draw the line at my old life. I was making endless plans - going places, seeing people, doing the housework, shopping, tea... trying to be a good 'housewife'- and for someone who hates cleaning, cooking and shopping, this was quite tough - I was killing myself. So much for the *'Sleep when the baby sleeps'* advice. I must have been insane. People offered to help. I had so many people around me but had never felt so alone in my life. The feelings were overwhelming to say the least. The nursery prison cell was my life. I spent all night trying to sleep and then all day unable to sleep.

As a first-time mum, how do you know if the *baby blues* are becoming more serious and where do you draw the line between poor mental health and sleep deprivation?

When the baby was seven weeks old, I was exhausted, delirious, desperate, happy and miserable. All at the same time. I sat on the beach and sobbed. My head was dark. The sun was shining but it was dark. My robotic experience of motherhood was not what I'd hoped for. The monotony of nappies, bottles, sick, poo, no poo, sick (again), was all consuming. Days ran into one and other. I was miserably happy. Lying to other people, to myself; creating a facade of happiness on Facebook. Pushing people away and feeling alone. Isolated but claustrophobic.

My life had to change. I had to slow down. I had to accept that I couldn't carry on the same way. I couldn't carry on living my crazy life with a baby in tow. Emilie had to come first. I had posted photos on Facebook of me looking 'fabulous' at two weddings and people had been so complimentary about motherhood suiting me... But I felt such a fraud. The 'fabulous' photos on Facebook didn't show how I was feeling. The days and nights were so hard and the desire to sleep and fantasies of sleep were all consuming. I was happy. But I was miserable too. How do you tell people that you aren't enjoying motherhood? That you secretly want your old life back? That even the thought of going back to work seems an easy alternative. Sleep deprivation has a lot to answer for!

I was diagnosed with post-natal depression at seven weeks and put back on antidepressants. I had been on them for many years and so they helped. But I helped myself as well. By accepting that I was different and finding the understanding and words to explain that difference helped. I started the blog *'The Little Book of Sick'* when she was ten weeks old and this was a turning point in not only my mental health, but my experience of motherhood.

Ultimately, I was also living in a life of cyclical abuse and didn't have the emotional support that I needed. But I am so glad that I sat on that beach and sobbed. I told people. Instead of hiding it and pretending that my Facebook life was real; I told people; I accepted help and slowly, my smiling darkness became a bloody exhausting beauty. The darkness lifted and I accepted my motherhood self and from that, my passion for writing began to blaze again.

## Write to Ignite

When Emilie was five months old, I went to *Blogfest* in London. To use the analogy, I surfed my way to London and felt my spark ignite. I went two years running, and in that room, surrounded by inspiring writers and speakers, I felt so at home.

I arrived full of hope and desperate for inspiration... I left full of inspiration and desperate to write.

A day for me. And I don't mean because I was a new mum and I enjoyed a day away from the baby – yes, that was a bonus - what I mean was a day to be the true me again. The me that had passion and desire to be a writer. The me that used to aspire to be a journalist, to write, to publish a novel. I always used to have this feeling and I hadn't felt it for such a long time. I was finally able to learn, to soak up every bit of information on offer.

My passion for writing was re-ignited.

I attended a guest expert masterclass *A Room of One's own: Motherhood and Creativity* and listened to Margaret Atwood (author of The Handmaid's Tale, which I wrote my dissertation on) speak about Motherhood and Creativity. I wanted to stand up and shout out and exclaim my joy and excitement at just being there and how motherhood had indeed reignited my spark by giving me time away from the pressures of teaching and the headspace to be creative again.

Meera Syal also spoke about the Punjabi belief of childbirth involving the birth of a new self... the mother self and how this mother self needs to be nurtured and celebrated. That is exactly how I felt. When I had my baby, something changed in me. Not only was a new baby born, a new mother was born. And I hadn't had a fucking clue how to deal with her.

Having now met and worked with Awena Naomie Ella, I have learned that what I went through - the physical, psychological and emotional changes women go through after the birth of your child have a name: matrescence. I didn't know it was a thing – I just thought I was selfish and not doing motherhood right! I wish I could go back and tell myself that everything was going to be okay.

*Blogfest* reminded me of the thrill and excitement that I used to feel every week when I drove home from my MA seminars, the thrill of writing, brainstorming, pitching, sharing and being creative. I wanted it so much but for twelve years, that life had been suppressed. I promised myself that I would write and set out plans for the book that I had always wanted to write. *The Little Book of Sick'* was pitched to several publishers with favourable responses but I never quite had the guts to go for it. I just hadn't fully learned how to get on that surfboard!

It was always meant to be and was achieved *All in Good Time*. My blog could have been successful, I could have written a book but I wasn't in the right personal space to do so. I was still surviving.

Procrastination and self-sabotage began to get in the way, with every excuse known to man coming up as a reason not to write. Why? Not because I don't want to but because of fear. Not just fear of publishing but the fear of what I would write. Being in that sense of flow is when my truth appears. My fingers type almost without my knowledge and my heart pours out, and along with it, years of supressed thoughts, feelings and trauma.

This is one of the big reasons why I stopped writing: fear of writing the truth. I was surviving in an emotionally abusive relationship. After being inspired at *Blogfest,* I sent off an article to *The Glasshouse Girls,* an online women's magazine. It was published, but not under my name and I didn't dare share it with anyone. My anger, hurt and deep unhappiness shone like beacon of desperation, but it was only shared with strangers. They even had to tone down one of my expressions of wanting to, '*Stab him in the eye*' as it was too violent. Nobody picked up the red flags, nobody saw my cry for help. I was terrified that someone would actually read it and not long after that, I stopped writing.

Until Lockdown. I reignited the blog, started to write again and my spark was re-lit.

## Stand with me Ignited

Launching my first published book was a ground-breaking moment and allowed me to put my surfboard into action and for once, literally, as it was the special guest at my book launch for people to surf on. My little book, *Time to Ignite – the 5-step mindfulness system,* is so special and has helped so many women to step away from mum-guilt and to set time for themselves – non-negotiable. The launch raised funds for *Oscar's Mission*, which was set up by my mummy-friend Becks Jones. Becks who I met as a new mum when living on the Wirral, lost her son Oscar in 2018 after he was stillborn at the Countess of Chester Hospital only a year after her mum died.

Becks was taking on a *Stand up Paddle board* mission in memory of Oscar and, as I love speaking about jumping on your metaphorical surfboard, and Becks was well and truly taking action and riding her board for her son, I wanted to get involved.

I interviewed Becks in my group and it was a big deal for her, to speak publicly about losing Oscar for the first time. I was so honoured to be able to share Oscar's story and say his name by raising extra funds via my book launch. The book went on to sell hundreds of copies and Becks and I were featured in the press surfing my ironing board together in the centre of Lymm, Warrington.

Publishing that book and receiving such amazing feedback allowed me to be able to tell my imposter syndrome to *'bugger off',* once and for all. I was doing it. I was a published author!

Writing is now my a big part of my job. As well as writing and publishing books, I write copy daily for emails and social media posts and I love that I can call myself an author and freelance writer. I proofread for Authors and Co and write professional media bios and press releases for Chocolate PR to help other women to share their stories in the media. Getting paid to write and feedback from clients saying, *'You are so talented'* and seeing your articles make the press is just everything.

The Louisa aged fourteen, who used to write for the school *Grapevine magazine* would be so proud that Louisa aged forty-two is doing what she bloody well loves! My purpose is to inspire and empower people, women, like you, who have been through your own share of adversity who are ready to say 'YES' to wanting more. Are you ready to open your *sliding door* and grab onto any opportunities that have passed you by? It is never too late.

Look inside yourself and listen to your purpose. It takes bravery and trust to really tune in and find that spark, but I promise you it is there and when you find it, it is so magical and that fire will roar inside of you. If you are in business, what do you stand for? What do you want to say?

Have a think about your business and these questions. You may have answered them before; read the questions and then close your eyes and look inside to what you really want to do, not what you think you should.

What is your purpose?

What is your mission?

Who do you want to help and inspire?

What is your why?

What do you want to be remembered for?

WHAT can you help people with?

WHY do you want to help them?

Getting clear on your purpose and message can take time and may very well evolve as you and your business do. Without a clear message you will confuse your ideal client. They need to see you as the expert and understand what you can help them with before you even worry about the how!

Think about what you want from your life, home, relationship or in your business. What do you want to say? What do you want to change? Are you ready to rise from the ashes?

## Chapter 8
# Rise

*"The difference between who you are and who you want to be is what you do."*

What are you passionate about? What annoys you? Where do you want to make a difference? What burns you up inside? This is your purpose! Using this passion to drive you forward is the key. If you are passionate about what you do, it will light you up and you will shine. Stepping into your passion and purpose so that your whole brand links to your purpose and passion. From passion comes fire, and once you have stepped into you power, you will begin to rise. It has taken some time, but I have risen from the ashes, stronger and more determined than ever.

When I stepped into my purpose and aligned the message of *Mamas Ignited* with the ironing board, I found my zone of genius. Expertise and qualifications are so important, but passion is everything and so much more. When you combine the two, this is where you find your zone of genius.

Now, I am not going to claim to be a brand specialist and if I am honest, until I was taken under the wing of one very special Fairy Godmother, JoJo Smith, I didn't know my pumpkin from my glass slipper. We were both on the *Bee Inspired* cohort together and she reached out to me for a chat, which turned into a SAS-Storm, which turned into me not sleeping for a bloody week with the number of ideas and excitement spinning round my head.

With her inner magic, Jojo had spotted my potential and need for a bit of steering in the right direction. I had only come up with the idea for my business a month before - it didn't even have a name - and she asked me to write down my Vision, Mission, Values and Message. Oh my god. Sixteen years of teaching and I was the dumbfounded student with not a clue. I felt like an absolute fraud. Who the hell was I to start a business? All those fears of judgement and imposter syndrome swamped me and I wanted to run back to the safety of my pile of books and keep marking for the rest of my life.

What the hell was mission? I had no clue.

And then I said... *"Well, I do have this one idea..."* and I told her about the ironing board. It was a winner. The surfboard was here to stay.

With the addition of the ironing board, I knew that my brand and message had to be about power! I couldn't sleep for days on end, journaling ideas through the night, voice noting Jojo at silly o'clock and then, after many drafts and redrafts, finally *Mamas Ignited* landed on my page and it was the one. I knew as soon as I saw it. Now, I am notorious for being indecisive and needing the world's validation for everything I do, but like when I named my baby Emilie... when I named my business, I just knew. *Mamas Ignited* held all the power, spark, flames, and catalyst that I wanted my business to stand for. Many people talk about the need for a strong personal brand and in the last year I have considered it, but *Mamas Ignited* is my mission. It is my vision and with it comes my message of power and strength that no matter what you have been through, you have the spark in you to ignite and you can be more, do more and have more without apology.

Soon the surfboard/ironing board became synonymous with my brand and with the help from CreativSAS and Rosie Wood, my stunning branding was launched and within only a few short months, I had a recognisable brand. Your brand is what people say about you and what they remember you for... it is not the colour of your logo. Your branding is a part of your brand but ultimately, you brand is *you*. I didn't understand this at first and I know from speaking to brand experts, that a lot of people make the mistake of having the branding take the lead.

You and your brand are what needs to take the lead in your message so that people remember you for what you want them to. People remember me as the lady with the ironing board, the surfing lady and I regularly get tagged and sent pictures of animals, kids, women surfing. I love it. My poor ironing board, not so much... the poor thing only gets dragged out for photoshoots and other than that stands redundant in the corner. Well, expect at Christmas when it makes an excellent wrapping station and buffet table!

## Stepping onto the Surfboard

When I joined the online space and began to carve out a business, I had no clue who I wanted to help. I kind of knew that I wanted to help other mums, possibly survivors of trauma, but I felt like an imposter. I had been a teacher for so long that I only knew how to teach.

Initially, my plan was to be a Relax Kids coach, but after signing up to *Bee Inspired* with Dani Wallace, I knew that I wanted so much more. I still work with Relax Kids in my local area and absolutely recommend the company 100%, but my path started to take a different course and almost like a calling, *Mamas Ignited* was destined to be.

When I was first asked by Dani why I wanted to speak and who I wanted to speak to, it was hard. Firstly, because I couldn't even imagine at that point that any audience would want to listen to me, let alone pay me for the privilege! I was already connected to Caroline Strawson and in truth, what she was doing was deep down what I wanted to do. But I knew that I didn't have the trauma informed training or counselling experience to even begin to put myself out there as an expert in the field of narcissistic abuse. I mean, I'd only just started to put myself back together again.

I joined another life-changing course, *One to Many with Lisa Johnson*. Again, I was very soon asked to describe my ideal client. If you haven't heard of Lisa Johnson, then I highly recommend that you check her out. I joined her challenge from my sick bed with Covid. I was ill for two weeks, with ten days being utterly dreadful. I was at home with a five-year-old, without any energy and the worst lethargy I have ever known. I was breathless going up the stairs and so I made a bed in the living room and we pretty much camped down there so that I was close to the kitchen (and thankfully, I have a downstairs loo.)

If I hadn't have had Covid, there's a strong chance that I would have missed Lisa's challenge and *Mamas Ignited* may not have been developed in the way it has. Listening to Lisa's lives each day gave me a literal spark of energy and excitement. I followed her tasks to the letter and enjoyed having the time to write in my notepad and do all of the things that she suggested. I knew that I had the potential to create something amazing. For once, my limiting beliefs left the building and I could see a clear vision of success. I could see myself leaving teaching and launching the business to run alongside the talk that I was working on delivering for Bee Inspired.

I knew that I had to give myself permission to leave teaching, to be more than be a teacher and despite my money mindset issues, I was able to allow myself to visualise a life where I was living a life with more abundance. I had to join the course. I was lucky that I had some money put away from a house sale and so I did it. Just like that. No discussing it with everyone I know. No seeking external validation... I made a decision and I went for it and I have never looked back.

## Finding my Igniters

When I first started *Mamas Ignited*, I wasn't entirely sure what I was going to do. I didn't feel like an expert in anything, but I knew my *why*. I wanted to help women who had been through adversity, women who wanted more but felt stuck in their lives.

For me, it was a feeling before it was a tangible thing. I had this urge and pull to change direction, to be more. I now know it to be my intuition, which wasn't something that I was aware of back then.

I started off playing safe and was looking at launching a mindful revision programme for secondary pupils. But in session two, Lisa's words hit me, *'Profit follows Passion'* and as I looked back at my list of all of my experience and expertise, and I knew who my audience were. I knew who my ideal client was.

It was me... but a few paces behind.

The woman that was trapped in an abusive relationship, the woman that had been seeking love and validation, the woman who needed to please, who was striving for acknowledgment at work, the woman that wanted more but had given up on her dream. My audience was a younger version of myself. The woman that gave up on her dream of being a writer and working in the media. The woman who became lost in her warped view of what it meant to be successful. The woman who had been hiding for way too long and was ready to follow her heart.

This was my audience. Women, namely mums, who had put up their ironing board and got a boring job. Women who had lost their desire to surf, women who want so much more from life.

*Mamas Ignited* was born.

## PR Powerhouse

Have you ever had your name in the paper? I was first in National paper when I was about two. I was called a *'Beautiful*

*Rose,*' as I'd been featured in modelling campaigns and was even the Johnson's baby!

I can remember my joy at school if I was featured in the local Warrington Guardian - when I won the Book Day fancy dress as Pippi Longstocking, Walking Day and for my GCSE results.

Last year, my story of surviving an abusive relationship was featured in the local paper, but this time, I did not have the same reaction. The story revolved around the fact that I'd published my story of overcoming abuse and with that was looking to inspire other women who had been through adversity. Seeing it in print made me feel sick. At that point, November 2020, *Mamas Ignited* was only an idea, a spark of an idea. Seeing my story in the paper was a real shocker and it could have gone one of two ways. Part of me wanted to shrivel away and hide, walking into school that day was horrific as I realised that people could have read the story.

I hadn't told anyone that I'd written the book until just before it was published. I was totally unable to be visible and to tell the people closest to me that I'd laid myself bare was terrifying. And then it was in the paper!

But I stepped into my fear and shared it on Facebook. People bought the book. We hit Number One on Amazon and then people started to message me saying how much I'd inspired them.

One lady, unknown to me, sent me a pivotal message. She said, *"I am your daughter, I witnessed my dad do the same to my mum... you are doing amazing things and with you she will be fine."*

Your story is an integral part of your message. Your ideal client is often a younger version of yourself, so think about what you would have wanted to hear when you were struggling or wanting more. Use your story to connect with your audience and message. If you have had to overcome adversity, be prepared to share your journey, but the key is to speak from the scar not the wound. When I came into business, I felt like I needed to tell everyone what had happened *to* me. By working on my message, I realised that what had happened *for* me was now serving me to help and inspire others, thus becoming my message:

---

*"You can choose to do more, be more and have more."*

---

By getting visible, I'd helped someone else. More messages came and from there, *Mamas Ignited* was no longer a spark of an idea. It was a mission. My Adversity had happened for me, so that I could help others.

I was making impact. I was surfing the waves and it felt great, but it was also terrifying to be public, to have my story online and know that my ex could possibly see and read about what I was doing. I was approached by two national journalists who wanted my story, but they wanted all the grit and the detail of the abuse and trauma, to name and print pictures of us as a *Happy Family* alongside photos of my bruises. This made me feel sick. Yes, I wanted to gain PR, but this felt all wrong.

Then, at the most perfect time, Jo Swann appeared in my life. I had seen her name listed as a bonus for Dani and knew that she was a PR specialist, but when she put out her *More than Media – Famous Five* mastermind, I knew I needed to be in her world.

Jo is only being mentioned late on in this book, but Jo has been the most instrumental part in helping me to rise and to step into my power, my authority and expert status. In every way, she supported me, pushed me, held my hand and showed me how to be unapologetically me and to take hold of my mission to empower other women like me, like you, who have suffered adversity but are ready to ride that surfboard.

My ironing board and I first appeared live on Jo's Live during one of our challenges and people still talk about when they saw me surfing the ironing board. That line, '*An ironing board is a surfboard that gave up on its dream...*' really was me, and Jo helped me to reclaim my surfboard and ride the waves of success.

Have a think about your story and the things that have happed *for you*. Tapping into the truth of your story and speaking from the heart is the best thing that you can do to reach and connect with your audience, and especially the media.

## Getting into the media

Getting into the press is a powerful way to create impact and to supercharge your business. You can have the best course and the most inspiring book, but if no-one knows about them then no-one will benefit from your expertise. Social Media is great for network building, but to establish yourself as an expert in your field, you need coverage by the media. Your content will also help to demonstrate your passion and purpose as the expert and authority in your field. Your story is everything in PR and connecting to your story and living aligned within your *why* is everything. If you haven't already, then checkout Jo Swann's podcast, *PR Powerhouse*. She will show you how you can claim your expert status and use your story for good.

Getting into the media in your early days of business is crucial to help to position yourself as an expert. Being in the media can super fast-track you so that your ideal clients trust and recognise you as the expert as you are demonstrating your credibility.

Believing in your true worth as an expert in your field is your first and most crucial step to getting press ready. You need to be clear in your messaging and mission; want to share your passion and purpose.

Working with Jo, alongside preparing for *Bee Inspired,* brought everything together for me. With Dani, I was working on my story, my message and how I wanted to use my talk to create impact, and Jo made sure that this impact created ripples to reach further afield. I was interviewed on the 'Andrew Pierce Daily Mail Podcast' for International Women's Day, featured in a wide range of online publications and quoted as an expert in several more.

The more I became visible, the more my passion grew and with that, the more the divide between my two worlds grew. During the six-month *Bee Inspired* Mastermind, I was still working part-time as a teacher. It was like being back in my *Sliding Door* life from my twenties again. In school, as Miss Herridge, I was back playing small, feeling the paranoia, judgement and anxiety. As Louisa from *Mamas Ignited,* I was strong, empowered and full of self-belief. I was supported by like-minded women who all knew how it felt to want more and to put a plan into action to make it happen.

When April came around and it was time for my talk at *Bee Inspired*, Covid restrictions meant that instead of speaking in a live venue in Manchester, we were instead moved to a studio in Coventry. This meant that I needed the time off work. I couldn't possibly commute to Coventry. I was part time so needed three hours covering. I asked for unpaid leave, explained the gravity of the situation, how it had been a huge part of my recovery from depression, how the event was supporting the *Fly Anyway Foundation*, that supports survivors of domestic abuse. It was refused. I was told that, despite the importance of the event, it was not possible to grant unpaid leave and that I had to make a choice between my priorities.

So, I did. I told him to stick his job and never looked back!

Making that decision was so easy, but so hard. I was a solo mum, and I was giving up a stable job during a pandemic, but my intuition, my gut told me that I just had to do it. I had to work my notice until the end of April, but I took the '*unpaid*' leave for *Bee Inspired* regardless, and it never felt so good.

I was driven to do it by something beyond head and heart. I just knew that I had *so* much more to do with my life and *so* much more that I wanted to be and, dare I admit, I wanted to have more. To have more freedom, more time, more options and more money. I was led by my gut and as a very wise friend told me, 'Your head can lie, your heart is a fool, but your gut is never wrong!'

The intense relief was palpable.

Teaching was so easy to leave. The only thing that made it hard to leave were the pupils. I cried about leaving my Year 11 pupils, I cried at the thought of never teaching *Romeo and Juliet* again, but the thing that made me the happiest was how proud my pupils were. I told them the truth about why I was leaving, my struggles with mental health and that I was leaving to write a book and create a coaching business supporting other women. My Instagram followers went through the roof when I left and I still have a few superfans! This is why I loved teaching, the bit that most people assume is the hardest is in fact the absolute best – nurturing young minds and inspiring them. I know that by leaving and following my passion, I have inspired many of those young people more than if I had stayed in a place that made me ill.

## Life was Simpler when Women knew their place

Choosing the ironing board as a part of my messaging meant that it was a no-brainer that when I spoke on stage at *Bee Inspired*, my ironing board would somehow feature. The creative process of writing the talk was one of my favourite projects. After teaching for so long, I absolutely absorbed every single bit of learning like an eager sponge.

I was still teaching and running the show as a single mum, so the evenings were my time for learning. It brought me to life. One of the reasons that I have loved my teaching career is that I love learning new things. Did you know that the average adult hasn't learned anything new for ten years? That is shocking, but all easily understandable. I hadn't read any non-fiction since I had been at university and there I was, at the age of forty-one, devouring everything in sight. I now struggle to read fiction as my thirst for knowledge and development is insatiable... plus, I know a lot of amazing authors now so there is always a fresh launch with another amazing read to be added to my pile.

Writing my talk for *Bee Inspired* allowed me to bring together my feminist standpoints, my own story with an uplifting message to the audience. It worked. Immediately afterwards, I had women in my inbox who empathised with what I had been talking about, victims of abuse and women who wanted more. All of these women have now become friends and clients. Speaking on that stage with passion and purpose was the moment that I was able to fully *rise* and feel the magnitude of what I had achieved in six short months.

I was a well-known brand, featured in national press, with a book on the way. As I stood on that ironing board and looked into the camera, I knew that I was reaching women, women like me who just needed the boost to know that it is possible. To know that anyone can change their mindset, their life and their happiness. But you have to accept that it is only you that can make it happen. You are responsible for you, but if you surround yourself with the right people, it's a whole lot easier.

# Chapter 9
# Empower

*"When you surround yourself with people who support your dreams, you will achieve success more quickly."*

Do you remember as a child, the gut-wrenching, heart sinking feeling right before you asked someone that you'd just met *'what is your name?'* The number of times I would be playing with a new friend, but just couldn't pluck up the courage to ask them. My mum and dad would encourage me, *'Just say 'My name is Louisa, what's yours?'* But I couldn't. It was too scary.

School, university, work, and now motherhood is where I have picked up my amazing mix of wonderful friends but back when I was a new mum, I was living in a new town, away from my family and I didn't have any friends at all. I needed friends more than ever.

I don't struggle to strike up a conversation. In fact, I talk to anyone. And I mean anyone - in the post office queue, in the playground, I can always spark a conversation. But how, as a grown up, do you say to someone *'Will you be my friend?'* without sounding completely desperate? I can remember walking around the park, trying to smile at other mums and desperately trying to 'make friends' to no avail.

Around this time, I'd started blogging and had had my eyes opened to the blogging community and the virtual online friends that were out there. I had a defining moment when I read a blog about how important it is to have Mummy friends. People had been telling me that it would all fit into place once I got some Mummy friends and into my new routine. But how did I meet people? I didn't even know where all of the groups were.

And then it hit me. I had the email addresses of all the women that I'd attended Hypnobirthing with. We all had babies around a similar age. Maybe they felt the same as I did. So, I did it. I put myself out there and sent an email and soon enough, I had a *Mummy Date*. We chatted, drank coffee and laughed. It was just what I needed. From there, I met more mummies and soon I had a network of friends. Six years on, Jen and her son, Ethan are still our besties and the life-jacket that we gave each other is still very much afloat.

Thankfully, since then, social media has become even more social, but it took until the first lockdown of 2020 for me to begin to find new friends again. Talking and connecting online has opened a whole new world to me. There are so many positive connections waiting to happen by meeting likeminded people online and I have forged so many wonderful connections and friendships in this crazy online space and thankfully, now I don't have to ask *What is your name...* well unless you are in real life networking! But it definitely is not scary anymore.

As a teacher, I always had friends across the whole school. Some teachers and departments can be very insular, but I have always been a lone wolf, not followed the crowd and my best work friends have always been outside of my own department. Being 'off sick' had become a trigger for my depression due to the extended amount of time that I have had off over the years due to my bad back and the pregnancy from hell.

When I hit the 'breakdown of December 2019', I was desperately trying to make it to Christmas because I knew that being on my own and having time to *just be* would create an avalanche of emotion that I had been desperately trying to avoid. I had got to the point with school that my paranoia was so bad, I didn't feel like I could trust anybody. I know that I upset some friends and colleagues as I had a mass exodus on Facebook and deleted many contacts. I was so angry that I was suffering and people didn't seem to care, but looking back with a rational head, people possibly didn't realise how bad I was or, due to the stigma attached to mental health, still didn't know how to speak to me. But even so, I had been cast adrift from the people who for months had been my daily sounding boards.

I busied myself with family, Christmas, and the antics of Tinky the Elf. I kept the tears at bay, I put on the happy mask. Even now, I can look back at smiling photos and fool myself about how I really was feeling. Depression doesn't mean that you can't be happy or enjoy yourself, but like your shadow, it is always there.

Once January hit, the gun crack fired that sent the avalanche cascading and I was immersed in ten years of trauma, pain, guilt and fear with not a shovel in sight.

Thankfully, one of my friends, Tanya, handed me a shovel and began helping me to dig myself out. She booked us tickets to the vision board workshop that I told you about in the *Receive* chapter. I spoke about how this day changed my life. I don't say that glibly, I was at a low that can't be fully articulated. I was in a freeze mindset, and the Louisa who had thrived in her career and life up until this point was at risk of disappearing all together.

That same night, I was offered free tickets to *Womanifest* from Emma Belmote, who was leading *Warrington Mums in Business*. I walked into the Hilton Hotel filled with excitement and the giggles. We drank our free champagne and I knew that my life had shifted on its axis again. The room was filled with women who were owning and bossing their lives. Up until that day, I had never believed that I could quit teaching and start my own business. For years, I had been haunted with the fact that I had quit writing, but finally, I was back in a place where I could admit that I wanted to *do more* and I knew that I was more than capable. The last time I had felt this spark was at *Blogfest* and there I was at *Womanifest,* ready to pack away that ironing board and to start living my life. The life that I was always ready to live.

That day not only gave me the boost to start my business, but it also opened up a world of friends, of connections that have been just as important in my recovery from depression and anxiety, finding my online people, this was just what I needed.

I joined Dani's online group, the *IATQB Hive*, but it still took me several months before I became active in there. The people that I met at *Womanifest* didn't jump into my life immediately, but I watched them from afar and the spark that lit inside me began to glow that day, and as each week and month went on it became stronger. As well as connecting with Dani, I connected with Deep Bajwa and I am delighted to be working with Deep and Dani in their *Amplify* Mastermind. As I write this, at the end of 2021, I knew that I wanted to invest again in my business, but this time from a strategy point of view.

In twelve months, I have come full circle. I am working with the two ladies who were my very first introduction to the online business world, the two women whose talks made me declare... *'Next year I will be on that stage.'* Deep's talk empowered me to step through my fear and *Take the First Step,* and Dani, as you already know, gave the hand to step into my own power, to *Show up, Wise up and Rise up.*

Now my online network of friends are just as important to me as my real-life friends. There are people that I speak to weekly, if not daily, and I have forged true friendships that I cherish.

In September, when I was sitting in the audience at *Bee Inspired,* at one point in the day I paused for a moment and scanned the room. I looked around and thought... *wow this is now my 'staff room'.* After sixteen years of teaching in pockets of misery, toxic environments and never being fully me in case it upset someone, being afraid to celebrate my achievements, being scared as a fucking English teacher to tell fellow English teachers that I'd written a book - the staff room was always a place of negativity. I was always a lone wolf in teaching, as I never quite fit in.

Now. I. Do.

I stand out, like we all do, as we do not need to fit in as we are all enough, just as we are!

This was MY ROOM. MY PLACE. MY PEOPLE. Full of positive, empowered, brave people who were not afraid to want more and to bloody well go for it.

After listening to all of such powerhouse, empowering women speak about taking the plunge, being brave. I knew that I had to bring a group of women together. Mamas who, like me, had been through some type of trauma, adversity, had dealt with pain, limiting beliefs and had lived a life that didn't make them happy, but have ignited their spark and are now thriving. Some of these women had no other choice. Life dealt them a blow where the slogan *What doesn't kill you makes your stronger* was the only way.

I did what I had felt compelled to do – to create a collaborative book. I had spoken to Abigail Horne at Authors & Co, back in June about my idea to run a collaboration, but *ye olde imposter syndrome* had convinced me that I needed to wait until next year. Why? Absolutely no reason. So, after *Bee Inspired*, I put the wheels in motion as I knew that this wasn't about selling, this was about putting out an offering that would change people's lives and it already has.

*From the Ashes: She is Ignited* is a collaboration showcasing the power of women to ignite and how, despite trauma and adversity, we can all find the inner power and strength to ignite and to rise from the ashes to live a new, stronger and empowered life. Who knows... maybe you will join my next collaboration?

I am honoured to be working with these women and it just goes to show how powerful the online network is. Through the power of social media, I have brought together women from across the world to write this book. Many of these women have connected with me during the rise of *Mamas Ignited* and so, by consistency, being visible, sharing my mission and showing up, it meant that when it came to joining my collaboration, these women already had the *Know, Like and Trust* factor with me. Many jumped in immediately as they had followed my journey and I am honoured that they chose to trust me.

The ripple effect of this online space goes beyond what you are selling or promoting in the here and now. How you make people feel, where you speak, what you say and how you say it will be remembered and will make ripples that you may not even be aware of... but if you stay consistent, talk the talk and importantly, walk the walk, these ripples will circle back to you.

With the Lockdown Zoom cloud starting to disappear it has been even more important to get out into the real world and carry on where I left off at *Womanifest*. Attending face-to-face networking events in the last six months has kickstarted my business in a totally different way. I have met new entrepreneurs, secured new alliances and made friendships alongside business connections. Turning up to an event with likeminded women is empowering and uplifting and I urge you to get out there and meet the people beyond the screen. I run my own IMPACT sessions and the chance to work on your business alongside other women is worth as much as the course itself – if not more.

Connection is everything, and I implore you to talk to and connect with as many people as you can. Introverts and extroverts alike can use this online rabbit warren to find your way into new fields, new worlds and the more you explore and make *genuine* connections, the more your message will resonate with people. Recently, somebody put on their status say what you do in five words, I wrote 'Chats shit for a living'. It was in jest but also so true, I chat to people all the time, people I have never met, people I admire and people that have made an impact on me. If I then make an impact on them, they tell their people and then their people find me and the ripples continue.

If we use social media to forge real, connected networks, then we are never lonely in this *'working for yourself business.'* It was very strange at first for me, working solo, but I am involved in so many spaces now and the ripples ebb and flow. Many of us are swimming in the same pond, which is fine as there is plenty of space for everyone to swim. The good thing about being in the same pond is that there are plenty of people to throw you a life raft and help to keep you afloat when you feel like drowning. I have never been as low as I was that day in the hot tub when I wanted the world to wash away. What I have gained from this tribe of people is the understanding that I am not alone. Other people have been through similar, worse or even unimaginable horrors and, due to these shared experiences, these friends have the ability to offer support, share experience and are role models for me as well. Women empowering women. It is magical.

When I look back at the new mum Louisa on maternity leave, who was so alone and lost, I wish I could tell her to just trust and believe and that everything would turn out exactly as it should be in the end. Saying *'Hello what's your name'* is no longer a fear, it is an opportunity to make a new connection and one that might change your life... or theirs!

## Live your 'Perfect'

As this book comes to a close I want to reflect on how my life has come full circle. For years I felt like something was missing when I was single. I was often lonely. Needing love and as such found that love in emotionally abusive relationships.

As a new solo mum when Emilie was two, I felt judged. Eyes on me. The *'single'* mum. I cried on our first few Christmases alone. Looked longingly at the *'Happy Family'* pictures on Facebook wishing it was me. I felt the odd one out on days out as a party of two instead of four.

I was so fixated on what I didn't have in my life that I overlooked what I did have. Now instead of focusing on what is missing I am grateful for the abundance that I have.

I have everything. Being mum to my amazing girl is everything. For a long time I thought she was missing out by not having her parents together. Then her dad disappeared from her life and I shouldered that guilt too. I had been looking for the perfect 2.4 family for so long, but I was looking at the picture all wrong.

Nothing is missing. We have everything. I am blessed with the love that I have.

We are the best team. She is the most grateful, kind, honest and wise little girl. She is clever, creative and makes me laugh.

I found the *'picture perfect'* family after all because there is no perfect. We are all surfing through life as best we can. But when we focus on the good it is a whole lot happier.

Emilie is my Happy Ever After.

# Epilogue

*"The Life you want is just within your grasp."*

I have always had wanderlust and I am very lucky to have travelled extensively as a child. Holidays were our happy place, where the five of us were invincible. I can only remember one big argument on a holiday as it was always the best of times when we were away. From countless holidays to Florida, we toured the USA, driving both coasts, the deserts - Vegas and Grand Canyon; exploring so many states and across the border to Canada and the wonder of Niagra Falls. We discovered untapped places like Vienna and Budapest, drove to the South of France and the Riviera and were often away in our caravan. Center Parcs was also a firm favourite, and this is in our blood as thankfully, now that my parents are happily divorced and friends, we have holidayed together as a family, which has meant so much to us.

Travelling is something that I will always do and I have my mum and dad to thank for this. They gave me that thirst for adventure and their parents gave them the same. Coming from working class backgrounds, they were both lucky to have parents who gave them wonderful experiences of other countries. We often hear about generational trauma, and I've spoken about childhood limiting beliefs. What I didn't highlight is the fact that my grandparents paved the way for my parents to give us the greatest of opportunities, dreams and experiences. Having all four grandparents until the age of thirty-seven, and still three with me as I publish this book, is so special. I am honoured to have known them as an adult and to have heard all of their stories of their lives. As children, we loved our grandparents so much but as an adult, I love them even more and I am so grateful for their influences on all of our lives. Losing my grandad was the hardest thing as it was my first brush with grief, but now I smile with the memories and the pride that he always had for me. He was a camper, a traveller and took my mum and uncle to Spain as children, which was unheard of at the time. He had many a tale to tell and his roving ways definitely have been passed on to me.

When the skies closed and we couldn't travel, I felt trapped. As a teacher, I had lived my life in countdown to the next holiday. Every single term was a countdown and that was how we all lived. Counting down with that never ending to-do list, judgement and scrutiny hanging over you. The holidays were always a plus to teaching and a source of much jeering from other people, but in many ways, the holidays were the worst thing. What I mean is that, by fixating on the holidays, I was always looking forward to the next thing that would make me happy. If I didn't have things booked, planned for the next few holidays, I would feel like there was no hope. Yes, I did do things in term time, but generally the *"We will do it in the holidays"* mantra meant that I was living an on-off existence. In the holidays, I didn't work… but that meant that I would have to work extra hard the week before and after the holidays.

At the time of writing this, it is the run up to Christmas and I worked a few shifts at the Christmas markets, on my friend's pretzel stand. One evening, I served an ex-teaching colleague. On seeing me serving pretzels he said, *"Wow this certainly beats teaching… couldn't think of a better place to work right now!"*

And he was right. I was there because I chose to be. I didn't need to be, my business was ticking over nicely, but I wanted to. I enjoyed chatting to people, serving and helping people to enjoy their night, I enjoyed the lights, Christmas music and the overall atmosphere.

It got me thinking about the usual *'Countdown to Christmas'*. Usually, I'd be so burnt out that I would be ill for the start of the holidays. Okay, I'm running low on fumes as I've been doing a lot lately, but no matter how exhausted I am, that spark is still in my eye and I am no longer counting down my life, begging for the next holiday.

I work for me and Emilie in the way that suits us.

I was still working four days before Christmas and there is no countdown because my life doesn't only exist in the holidays, like it used to. I live ALL the time. And it is bloody marvellous!

The flight embargo meant that I had to find a new way to live. I could no longer keep myself happy and excited by looking forward to the next holiday. For the first time in my life, I began to live in the moment. Since Lockdown One, I have found not having a holiday to be strangely liberating. For years,

I had been skint whilst saving up for a much-needed holiday and although I don't regret a single one, I have enjoyed our UK based holidays just as much in the last two years. The one thing I have missed is the promise of sunshine, but after achieving an incentive for ticket sales for *Bee Inspired* this year, I had the Autumn sunshine of Marrakesh and it was so much more than a holiday.

## The Magic of Marrakesh

I didn't believe I was going until I was sitting on that plane, ready for take-off. I hadn't been abroad for two years so not only was I visiting a country that I'd never been to before; I was finally getting back on a plane. Being away with 21 other women was so empowering; the sessions I attended, the conversations I had and the space and time I had to be alone helped me to make breakthroughs surrounding my own health, personal development and past traumas. For the first time, I realised how much I still relied on external validation and the fact that I was never broken.

I found myself on *self-love island,* in an oasis of calm, set against the bustling city which was a bombardment to the senses. It was exhilarating.

I travelled solo and for the first time since becoming a mum, I went away for five days, and in term-time, which meant I could stick two fingers up to teaching! This wasn't just five days away from being mum, this turned out to be five days to reconnect with the old Louisa. The Louisa who travelled across the globe solo, the one who had a thirst for travel, culture and adventure – the one who hadn't endured the pain, adversity and abuse. I found the Louisa from the top of the Sydney Harbour Bridge again and this time, I found her at the top of the Atlas Mountains.

Our day trip to the waterfalls didn't quite go as planned and instead of a nice walk, swim and lunch as expected, we ended up doing a four-hour trek up the Atlas Mountains to a mountain waterfall. If I had been told beforehand what it would entail, I am certain that I wouldn't have gone. My limiting beliefs would have told me that I wasn't fit enough, that it was too dangerous, that I didn't have the right shoes (I didn't) and I would have opted for a day in the sun with my book. Walking blind and being faced with this almighty challenge awoke something in me that had been lying dormant.

Climbing was tough. There were some very fit women amongst us, some who struggled more than me and a range of ages but we all bloody did it. We climbed through mountain villages, pop up shanty towns snuggled in the mountains. We climbed side-by-side with mountain goats, skirted sheer drops and every step was an almighty push. I kept the peak in sight, partly in disbelief, partly to focus as we carried on. I was out of breath in parts, strong and determined in others, but I was doing it and never once thought that I couldn't. Unlike the Louisa on the Sydney bridge, I was fearless and confident that I would succeed.

When we reached the waterfall, the sense of euphoria was on par with childbirth. The rush of oxytocin and feeling of being so fully alive was palpable. The waterfall was busy, filled with locals and tourists. I stripped down to my bikini, let my pasty white belly and thighs free and stood under that waterfall in all my size twenty glory. That was the Louisa from the top of the bridge, the woman filled with hope and passion, but this woman had carried far more to the top of the mountain. I had been carrying the weight of years of trauma, adversity and pain, but in that moment, at the top of that mountain in ice cold water, I was weightless. I was limitless. I was free in mind and free to be the woman that I was meant to be. I can take on anything, I can be anything and I know my authentic self. Climbing that mountain awoke a spirit in me for adventure, for risk taking and more importantly, acceptance of myself just as I am.

I learned so much about myself that week: that I no longer need to seek external validation, my choices are mine to choose and this new life has been created by me, for me, and I am so grateful. I left Marrakesh knowing what I want from life, who I want in that life and more importantly, who I am.

I am a mum, a coach, a speaker and an author. I am vulnerable. I am strong. I am passionate. I am proud. I am grateful. I am free.

I am Louisa Fucking Herridge, the leader of the *Mamas Ignited* movement.

I am ignited, surfing the fire of life, and you can too.

Stop ironing, start living.

On we bloody well surf!

# Acknowledgments

**My Mum and Dad who never stopped me dreaming**

My happiest memories as a child are our countless holidays to Florida when the magic of Disney meant that anything was possible. You gave me everything as a child and still now, as an adult, and I love you both. You have always believed in me and that is all I can ask for.

**Kelly and Adam - how lucky I am**

For all the times I was reading while you played Crash Bandicoot, now I can finally dedicate my book to you. You are my true soul mates with your unwavering support, love, laughter, and friendship.

**Sue, Sam & Lauren**

How were you ever not in my life? You are all so special with the love and happiness that you bring to our whole family.

**Nancy and Benjamin**

Being Aunty Louisa is the best job! I love you both so much. Never stop dreaming!

## Grandad in Heaven

How proud you would be. The most pessimistic optimist and dreamer to grace this earth.

## Grandma

You always said I would write a book one day! You have forever been my cheerleader.

## Nanna and Grandad

Thank you for your never-ending love, pride, and encouragement for everything that I do. Your support is never-ending.

## Dani Wallace

From the first time I heard your audacious statement *'I am the Queen Bee'* I knew I would #FLYANYWAY under your wing. We have so much more to do together. This is only the beginning!

## Jo Swann

For all of your support, giddiness and PR knowhow. You had my back from day one and saw my potential and you were the only person that I could ask to write the foreword. Thank you for just getting me.

## Jo Maloney

Your positivity is infectious and I love learning from you.

## Jojo Smith aka CreativSAS and Rosie Wilkins

For my stunning branding – you brought Mamas Ignited to life. #Wishesintoreality.

**Abigail Horne, Lucy Crane** and all the team at **Authors and Co.**

For helping me to achieve this lifelong goal.

**Lisa Johnson and team**

For giving me not just the tools to launch a business but the belief and support to succeed as an affiliate and in my own launches.

**Niki Kinsella**

You were one of the first people that I connected with. You have an aura around you that empowers me to be the best version of me.

**My *Bee Inspired* cohort**

You lifted me up, supported me and held me as I started this amazing journey.

**My first cohort of clients on SPARKS & IMPACT**

You have jumped on your ironing boards and are already creating ripples.

**Rachel Davies, Amie Blayney** and **Jo Wildsmith**

For being my beta readers and my team of true #IGNITERS

**Jenny Riley-Jenkins** and **Alex Gayward**

Not just for being my friends but for supporting me at every step of my journey as my clients.

**Sarah Howarth**

My lifelong reading friend. From swapping book and dreaming

of being writers to teaching English together - I couldn't have asked for a better debut reader.

## Emma Fowers

The Samantha to my Carrie, my lobster and best friend in the world (I'm talking behind the tennis ball).

## Michelle, Mark and the twinnies

Thank you for helping me out with childcare to get this book written!

## Jen and Ethan

Long live the devil and the diva.

## My online support network of #IGNITERS

You have been loyally cheering and supporting me on this crazy journey.

And finally I'd like to acknowledge **you... the reader**.

This is your first step to choosing to be more. You have the spark in you... never let it dampen.

# Useful Links

## Mental Health

MIND www.mind.org.uk
Samaritans www.samaritans.org
CALM www.thecalmzone.net

## Children's Mental Health

Relax Kids www.relaxkids.com
Young Minds www.youngminds.org.uk

## Domestic Abuse

National Domestic Abuse Helpline
www.nationaldahelpline.org.uk
Women's Aid www.womensaid.org.uk

# Work With Louisa

Thanks so much for reading and I would love to find out about your journey. Jump on those ironing boards, take a photo and tag me in your posts

**#MAMASIGNITED**

**#SISL**

**#SURFTHEFIRE**

## Join the Mamas Ignited movement

Surf my website for full details on books, collaborations, courses, speaking and more.

**Web:** www.mamasignited.co.uk

**Email:** info@mamasignited.co.uk

## Work with me and join the waitlist for my next course here:

https://mamasignited.co.uk/work-with-louisa/

# Download my free guide '*6 Steps to Ignite your Business Impact*'

Plus you'll get my **BONUS QUIZ** to find out which element you are living in.

EARTH | FIRE | WATER | AIR | SPACE

https://mamasignited.co.uk/6-steps-to-ignite-your-business-impact/

## Find me on all the socials

facebook.com/mamasignited
instagram.com/mamasignited
linkedin.com/in/mamasignited

Printed in Great Britain
by Amazon